I0266043

RISE, ANDALUS
The Fall of Imperial Harlotry

قومي يا أندلس

RISE, ANDALUS
The Fall of Imperial Harlotry

Marc Philip Boulos

OCABS PRESS
ST PAUL, MINNESOTA 55107
2025

RISE, ANDALUS
The Fall of Imperial Harlotry

ISBN 1-60191-065-7

PRINTED IN THE UNITED STATES OF AMERICA

Rise, Andalus
The Fall of Imperial Harlotry

ISBN 1-60191-065-7

Published by OCABS Press, St. Paul, Minnesota.
Printed in the United States of America.

Books are available through OCABS Press at special discounts for bulk purchases in the United States by academic institutions, churches, and other organizations. For more information, please email OCABS Press at press@ocabs.org.

To the Basement Crew,
helpers of God.

To Father Paul and Father Tim,
who bore witness in the darkness
and did not look away.

And to John Barnet,
Professor of New Testament Greek,
who gave me the most important lesson of all:
a grade I did not earn.

Foreword

Most people are familiar with the aphorism "history is written by the victors," but what does that say about history as a reliable account of what actually happened? Can our stories about the past be trusted? Are the voices of the vanquished lost forever? Fortunately, it is hardly the case that objective history is ever wholly obliterated. The story of what actually happened can—and, I would say, must—be recovered and reconstructed by critical historians who apply their methods to the fractured, distorted remains embedded in the dominant narratives that color our view of the world. Case in point, the history of al-Andalus, a name that derives from the Vandals, a Germanic tribe that migrated south of the Pyrenees, which became home to a magnificent Islamic culture that thrived between the 8th and 15th centuries and whose history was all but eclipsed by Spanish nationalist historians. It raises the question of whether propagandistic nationalist myths such as that of the glorious Reconquista be allowed to erase the history of a legitimate civilization and its rich culture? Fortunately, critical scholarship of the sort we find in this monograph can challenge this idea and recover suppressed voices that, in turn, can crack the brittle veneer of dominant earthly power, and even that of empire.

The Andalusian era was effectively brought to an end in 1492, when King Ferdinand and Queen Isabella issued the Alhambra Decree, a royal edict that called for the immediate expulsion of Jews from Spain and the confiscation of their property unless they agreed to convert to Christianity. For Muslims, the persecution was less immediate and more complicated, especially since al-Andalus was an Ummayad society. However, the expulsion and forced conversions of both groups had the same result, namely the all-but-complete eradication of Andalusian religion, dress, languages, and customs from the peninsula.

Ironically, the boons the latter had bequeathed to the West included rediscovered Aristotelian and other philosophical works, Arabic numerals (imagine an engineer trying to work with Roman numbers!), algebra (*al-jabr*), medical knowledge, and so on, all of which served to enlighten and inspire great European intellectuals like Thomas Aquinas and others. But what largely survives are fragmented works embedded in the triumphalist story of Empire, alongside exquisite architectural remains that stand mute before the magnificent omnipotence of God: Granada's breathtaking Alhambra, the Great Mosque of Córdoba (Mezquita), the Alcázar of Seville, and others. Meanwhile, Jewish thinkers from this intellectual golden age—doctors, poets, philosophers, and Scripture scholars such as Moses Maimonides ("Rambam"), Samuel ha-Nagid, Solomon ibn Gabirol, Hasdai ibn Shaprut, and others—bear witness through their enduring works.

The intellectual collaboration and mutual respect on the part of rational, God-fearing Jews and Muslims united in purpose by Scripture was all but brought to an end even as the so-called Renaissance was beginning. The extent to which Islamic and Jewish learning contributed to the Renaissance is debated among scholars, but it indisputably carried within itself the antidote to the excessive egoism and hubris of the classical works so prized by self-aggrandizing Europe. Toward that end, the present work finds potent medicine in the inherently rebellious power of the Semitic consonantal triliteral root, which challenges human systems in an equalized leveling that leaves only the possibility of submission to the will of the one God. In the end, according to Boulos, the expulsion from al-Andalus was not an extinction, but a "divinely ordained scattering" of the teaching of obedience to God and embrace of neighbor (197).

This thesis is demonstrated throughout the rest of the work through a number of brilliant "word and branch" studies, each one a lesson in itself, but assembling to demonstrate the assertion that in the consonantal triliteral root is conveyed all the knowledge, beauty, and power of Semitic expression, permitting a linguistic ambiguity that intensifies hearing within a certain "constellation of function" (25). Boulos offers as example the Semitic root *k-t-b* ("to write"), which underlies Arabic words like *kitab* ("book"), *kātib* ("writer"), *maktab* ("office"), *maktūb* ("that which is written"), and in Hebrew, words like *katub* ("written"), *miktab* ("letter"), and others (24-25). Here we see that the consonantal triliteral root not only shoots its semantic rhizomes throughout Hebrew and throughout Arabic but functionally unites them in both the Bible and the Qur'an. The effect here—the major thesis of this monograph—is that the consonantal triliteral root system resists abstraction, defies human ideologies and institutions, and makes available obedience to the shared God of Scripture and true liberation from the bondage of Self.

Foreword

Finally, a word about the culmination of this insightful foray into an all-but-forgotten world and what it might mean for all peoples today. Of course, hearing and understanding Scripture in its original form is lost to most of us, but the power of its central concept—that God is God, not us—is not lost, but preserved through the Greek translation of the Hebrew Bible, the Septuagint, produced a little over three centuries before the New Testament and which along with Aramaic (a Semitic language) informed the world of the New Testament. Boulos, who hears the gospel of Luke especially in this way, insightfully refers to the Septuagint as the "lexical spine"—the nerve center, if you will—of the Word of God to all Abraham's seed, transmitted over the synapses of time and geography regarding how we are to be in the world as children of the Most High God. Boulos indicates Luke's table fellowship as a reminder and the key. More than a metaphor, it must become a reality as it was long ago in an inextinguishable place and time. – Nicolae G. Roddy

About the Author of the Foreword

Dr. Nicolae G. Roddy is Professor of Theology at Creighton University in Omaha, where he specializes in the Hebrew Bible and Old Testament. He has served as Visiting Professor of Archaeology at the University of Bucharest and is co-director of the Bethsaida Excavations Project in Galilee. An accomplished scholar and teacher, Dr. Roddy brings together scriptural insight, archaeological fieldwork, and a lifelong dedication to understanding the biblical text in its historical and literary contexts.

Preface

In this sequel to *Dark Sayings,* I lay bare the first fruits of a journey born of both darkness and encounter. As the son of immigrants and refugees from the Middle East, since childhood, I have wrestled with rejection and erasure that cast its shadow over every corner of life. And yet, it was precisely in that darkness that a moment of divine clarity illuminated the truth of Abrahamic slavery and submission to him.

In Istanbul, hand in hand with the wife who walks beside me, I heard the recitation of the Noble Qur'an and watched the Sufi clerics whirl in devotion. And when the imam proclaimed, *Ṣadaqa Allāhu al-ʿAẓīm,* (صَدَقَ الله العَظِيمُ, "God Almighty has spoken the truth") it was as though the many threads of my years of biblical study—of the interwoven power of Hebrew and Arabic—suddenly converged.

In God's Semitic languages, the roots ص-ل-ح (*ṣād-lām-ḥā'*) and צ־ד־ק *(ṣade-dalet-qof)* intertwine righteousness, moral conduct, reconciliation, and the common good within a single grammatical tree of life, so that every correspondence echoes and reinforces the divine standard spoken once for all: that righteousness comes from God alone, who measures, perfects, and grants authority to every human act of justice, truth, reform, and prophetic utterance.

God found me wandering in my darkness, just as he has found so many before me, through the luminous bridge of his divine languages.

This book is my testament of gratitude: to him alone, and to the legacy of the scholars of al-Andalus, who understood long ago that the Arabic of the Qur'an and the Hebrew of the Bible are not rivals, but companions. They are keys to a shared understanding that has been silenced for too long.

And so, as you read, know that these pages carry the voice of someone who was found by light in that convergence, offering it now in gratitude and hope, *in the name of God.*

– Marc Philip Boulos

Note to the Reader

The chapters that follow
are written in the cadence of Scripture:
dense, poetic, lexical, uncompromising.

They are meant not only to be read
but to be heard—
unsettling as much as they instruct.

This is not a text to be skimmed.
It resists simplification.
It requires patience,
attention,
endurance.

At times you will want to put it down.
That is as it should be.
The path of wisdom is not easy.

To read is to wander in the dark,
to stumble and wait,
until the light comes.

Do not rush.
Do not flee.
The labor is the reward.

Patience in the struggle
is the only way to be found,
not by this book,
but by him.

Table of Contents

Foreword **11**

Preface **15**

Note to the Reader **17**

Part I
"Rise and stand upon the path of the Command" **21**
In the Name of God **23**
Rise, Andalus **33**
Ulamā' al-Andalus **35**

Part II
"Go into the wilderness of pasture" **71**
Human Evil is Not Banal **73**
The Voice of the Shepherd **105**

Part III
"Return repentant to the abode of mercy" **125**
The Desert Knows His Name **127**
Incense and Ash **165**
Word From a Mother **189**
The Borderless Table **193**
Word of the Three Scrolls **207**

Epilogue: Lift Up Your Gates **209**
The Shepherd Returns........209
The Septuagint as Lexical Spine........213
Our Semitic Roots........234
The Church Will Not Abandon Her Children........245

From al-Andalus to Gaza: Scripture Against Empire **249**
About the Author........250

Appendix: Hebrew Transliteration and the Palm Tree Initiative **251**
The Consolation of Consonants........251

Part I

قم وانصب على درب الأمر

qum wa-nṣib ʿalā darb al-amr

"Rise and stand upon the path of the Command"

In the Name of God

بِسْمِ ٱللّٰهِ إِلُ إِيلُوهِ نُوذِينَا

(bismi llāhi ilu īlūhi nūdhīnā)[1]

IN THE NAME OF GOD, El, Elohim, our Lord, we dedicate [this work] to him, seeking refuge in him,[2] in the shadow of 1492, when Ferdinand and Isabella expelled the Jews and Muslims from Spain and dispatched Columbus across the Atlantic, when a deeper memory from the Levant and North Africa persisted quietly beneath the surface. This memory wasn't encoded in the proclamations of kings or the movements of imperial fleets, but in the enduring logic

---

[1] Jonah Ibn Janāḥ. *Kitāb al-Uṣūl*, edited by Adolf Neubauer, Oxford, Clarendon Press, 1875, p. 91. The phrase "بِسْمِ ٱللهِ إِلُ إِيلُوهِ نُوذِينَا" *(bismi llāhi ilu īlūhi nūdhīnā)* echos Daniel 2:23, used in Ibn Janāḥ's comparative Semitic analysis. The invocation بِسْمِ ٱللهِ (*bis-mi-llāhi*, "In the name of Allah") connects to the divine name إِلُ (*i-lu*), derived from El, while إِيلُوهِ (*i-lū-hi*) is cognate with the biblical Elohim plus the possessive suffix *-hi*, literally "my God," and نُوذِينَا (*nū-dhī-nā*) from نَذَا *(nadhā*, "to dedicate" or "to vow" is functional with the Hebrew נָדַר, *nadar*, "to vow" or "to promise", *eg.* Numbers 30:3) or عَاذَ *('ādhā*, "to seek refuge" eg. "قُلْ أَعُوذُ بِرَبِّ ٱلنَّاسِ مَلِكِ ٱلنَّاسِ إِلَٰهِ ٱلنَّاسِ", *qul a'ūdhu bi-rabbi-n-nāsi maliki-n-nāsi ilāhi-n-nāsi,* "Say: I seek refuge in the Lord of mankind, the King of mankind, the God of mankind." From سورة الناس, Sūrat an-Nās 114:1-3, the final chapter of the Qur'an.), hence "we dedicate [this work] to him, seeking refuge in him."

[2] Ibid.

of language: the triliteral root system of the Semitic scrolls.

Hebrew and Arabic share a grammatical core rooted in three-letter consonantal anatomies. Yehuda Ḥayyūj (يهوذا الحَيُّوج, c. 945-1000), of al-Andalus, was the first to emphasize the significance of triliteral roots, but it was Yonah Ibn Janāḥ (يونه ابن جناح, c. 990-1050), also of al-Andalus who fully documented the Lord's grammar, developing a definitive methodology that shaped both Biblical and Qur'anic linguistic scholarship. [3] This triliteral system is not merely a linguistic curiosity; it is a datum, an irreducibility, an organ of divine grammar. The root ك-ت-ب (*kāf-tāʾ-bāʾ*) in Arabic spawns a

[3] Abū al-Walīd Marwān ibn Janāḥ (أبو الوليد مروان بن جناح), also known in Hebrew as Yehudah ibn Janāḥ (יְהוּדָה אִבְּן גַּ'נָאח), was an 11th-century Jewish physician, grammarian, and lexicographer from al-Andalus, most likely based in Zaragoza. A key figure in the Judeo-Arabic intellectual tradition, Ibn Janāḥ advanced the groundbreaking claim, most fully articulated in his *Kitāb al-Tanqīḥ*, that the Hebrew language could not be adequately understood without reference to Arabic. Drawing on the tools of Arabic philology, he situated Hebrew within the broader context of Semitic linguistics, treating Arabic not only as a sister language but as a necessary interpretive lens for biblical exegesis. His method was later corroborated, centuries afterward, by the Orthodox biblical scholar Paul Nadim Tarazi, who argues that "biblical Hebrew" was not a native language per se, but rather a scriptural dialect formulated from the extant Semitic tongues of the Mesopotamian region. Tarazi emphasizes that the Qur'an's unique role in preserving the structure of Arabic grammar makes it indispensable for understanding biblical Hebrew on a linguistic and historical level. In this way, Ibn Janāḥ's early philological intuition finds modern affirmation in a broader scholarly tradition that views the Semitic languages as deeply interdependent, both in structure and in their scriptural transmission.

constellation of function around writing: كتاب (*kitab*, "book"), كاتب (*kātib*, "writer"), مكتب (*maktab*, "office"), مكتوب (*maktūb*, "that which is written"). Its Hebrew parallel כ-ת-ב (*kaf-tab-bet*) yields כָּתוּב (*katub*, "written"), מִכְתָּב (*miktab,* "letter"). Hearing is shaped not through imposed categories but through use, syntax, and command.

This system resists abstraction. It resists theologies that demand metaphysical scaffolding and philosophies that prioritize systems over Scripture. It grounds thought in action, hearing in utility, and interpretation in shared linguistic function. As such, it provides not merely a medium for communication, but a grammar, not of community or relationship (the propaganda of Los Trastámaras)[4] but of radical submission.

In al-Andalus, the Maghreb, and West Asia, this triliteral inheritance made inter-religious scholarship not only possible but natural. Muslim scholars wrote about Hebrew grammar. Jewish scholars authored Arabic lexicons. Christian thinkers borrowed structural insights from both traditions. *Kitāb al-Uṣūl* (كتاب الأصول, *The Book of Roots*), by Ibn Janāḥ, a Hebrew lexicon composed in Arabic, revolutionized lexicographical scholarship by establishing a unified methodological framework that integrates etymology, comparative

---

[4] The Trastámaras were a Castilian dynasty that rose to power in 1369 when Henry II defeated his half-brother, Peter I of Castile. Originating from the title Count of Trastámara in Galicia, the dynasty eventually ruled both Castile and Aragon. Its most famous figures, Isabella I of Castile and Ferdinand II of Aragon, completed the Reconquista and unified Spain, after which their heirs brought the Spanish crown into the Habsburg line.

linguistics, morphology, semantics, cultural context, and textual criticism.

It is this tradition, this way of hearing, of submitting, of encountering (not experiencing) God through shared roots rather than human hierarchies, that was disrupted by the arrival of European empire. With the fall of Granada, the issuance of the al-Ḥambra[5] Decree, and the imposition of forced conversions, the good and perfect gift of Semitic cooperation come down from above was violently fractured.[6] In 1492, Jews were ordered:

> *"To depart from all of these our said realms and lordships... under pain that if they do not perform and comply with this command... they incur the penalty of death and the confiscation of all their possessions." (al-Ḥambra Decree, 1492)*[7]

In 1502, Queen Isabella outlawed Islam in Castile, demanding Muslims convert or be expelled. The same pattern would repeat in Aragon. Language, dress, ritual,

---

[5] الحمراء (*al-Ḥamrā'*) "The red one," referring to the reddish color of the walls and towers of the famous palace complex in Granada, Spain.

[6] The Reconquista was the centuries-long campaign by Christian kingdoms to reclaim the Iberian Peninsula from Muslim rule, culminating in the fall of Granada in 1492 and the dissolution of nearly 800 years of Semitic coexistence in al-Andalus.

[7] Ferdinand II of Aragon and Isabella I of Castile. *The Alhambra Decree (Edict of Expulsion of the Jews)*, March 31, 1492. Translated by Edward Peters, in *The Jew in the Medieval World: A Source Book, 315-1791*, edited by Jacob Rader Marcus, Hebrew Union College Press, 1999, pp. 220-224.

and memory were all to be purged.[8] The divine memory of the region—the grammar of difference, the syntax of coexistence—was replaced by the theological machinery of empire.

Isaac Abravanel, a Jewish scholar and treasurer to the monarchs, wrote of the people's anguish:

> *"When the dreadful news reached the people, they mourned their fate, and wherever the report of the decree spread, Jews wept bitterly."*[9]

Just three centuries earlier, the al-ʿAyyāḍiyyah (العيّاضية) massacre of 2,700 prisoners after the Siege of ʿAkkā (عكّا) in 1191, ordered by Richard the Lionheart of England[10] during the Third Crusade, marked a

---

[8] In 1478, with papal authorization from Pope Sixtus IV, Isabella I of Castile and Ferdinand II of Aragon, both of the Trastámara dynasty, established the Spanish Inquisition under direct royal control, appointing Tomás de Torquemada as first Grand Inquisitor in 1483. Initially aimed at conversos suspected of secretly practicing Judaism, it later targeted Muslims and others, becoming a central tool of religious uniformity. In 1492, the year they completed the Reconquista with Granada's conquest, they issued the Alhambra Decree expelling Jews and sponsored Columbus's first voyage. See Henry Kamen, The Spanish Inquisition: A Historical Revision, 4th ed., Yale University Press, 2014, pp. 10,43 56-64, 88-92; and Peggy K. Liss, Isabel the Queen: Life and Times, Oxford University Press, 1992, pp. 142-147, 162-163, 197-231.

[9] Ibn Verga, Solomon. *Shevet Yehudah (The Scepter of Judah)*. Translated by Cecil Roth, Jewish Publication Society, 1946.

[10] Richard the Lionheart (1157-1199), also known as Richard I of England, remains one of the most iconic and romanticized figures of the medieval period. Yet his orchestration of calculated terror, most notably the mass murder of Muslim prisoners at ʿAkkā, stands in stark contrast to tales of Christian virtue and noble warfare that surround his legacy.

threshold to the modern world, just two years before the death of Ṣalāḥ ad-Dīn (صلاح الدين, "Righteousness of the Faith") in 1193. The logic was the same: erase the Semitic other to secure imperial order. From the slaughter in Palestine to the expulsion of Jews in 1492, and the forced conversions of Muslims a decade later, the arc of European Christendom bent toward a colonial theology that erased the Semitic texts—Arabic and Hebrew alike—replacing the grammar of coexistence with a language of dominion. This was the trajectory that laid the groundwork for contemporary Western liberalism: a campaign not only of land, but of language, memory, and the systematic unmaking of coexistence.[11]

What emerged in place of Semitic memory was the imperial melting pot: a totalitarian identity masquerading as unity. Where the ancient Semitic tradition cultivated plurality through shared roots,

---

[11] This historical framing draws from a personal conversation with Dr. Nicolae Roddy, August 1, 2025. The massacre at Ayyadieh, in which Richard I of England ordered the execution of approximately 2,700 Muslim prisoners after the Siege of ʿAkkā (Acre) on August 20,1191, is documented in both Latin and Arabic sources, including the *Itinerarium Peregrinorum et Gesta Regis Ricardi* and the writings of Baha ad-Din ibn Shaddad. The ideological continuity from this event to the 1492 expulsion of Jews from Spain and the later forced conversions of Muslims reflects a broader shift from convivencia to a colonial theology of dominion. See also Maalouf, Amin. *The Crusades Through Arab Eyes.* Translated by Jon Rothschild, Schocken Books, 1984; Cohen, Mark R. *Under Crescent and Cross: The Jews in the Middle Ages.* Princeton UP, 1994; Menocal, Maria Rosa. *The Ornament of the World: How Muslims, Jews, and Christians Created a Culture of Tolerance in Medieval Spain.* Back Bay Books, 2002.

empire sought conformity, relationship, and community through enforced sameness. It imposed unifying identities: Catholic, Christian, Western, white, secular, nationalist, democratic, and pluralistic that erased distinctions that God, himself, our Shepherd—his name alone be praised—had ordained in his divine languages, unknown to the Europeans, who to this day persist in their violent worship of Greek things, spoken in the languages of law, tenure, commerce and war.

The Semitic root tradition is, by contrast, a grammar of difference and surrender. It is multilingual by nature, trans-religious from the fleshly womb, (where it is found, according to the Master's will) anti-totalitarian, and thus, anti-democratic, as it was created. It functions not as a closed system, but as a network of connections: the Hebrew ק-ד-ש (*qof-dalet-šin*, "set apart") echoes in the Arabic ق-د-س (*qāf-dāl-sīn*, "holy"); the Hebrew ש-מ-ע (*šin-mēm-ʿayin*, "hear") reverberates with the Arabic س-م-ع (*sīn-mīm-ʿayn*, "listen"). The root structure itself presupposes not relationship, a word lusted after by the harlots of empire, but function, a term of duty and action.

Empire, on the other hand, presupposes control. It converts difference into threat and multiplicity into violence. It defines peace as sameness and justice as assimilation. It flattens the garden of languages and peoples into monoculture. But the God of Scripture is not the god of empire. God scattered the languages at Babel. God called Abraham to be the father of many peoples. God gave each people their tongue, their name, and their wandering in his care in the open field, free from the tyranny of tower builders.

Thus, the triliteral womb of the Semitic tradition remains steadfast as an act of resistance صمود (*ṣumūd*), [12] not only to imperial power but to the philosophies and theologies that paved the way for it. الله الصمد (*allāhu ṣṣamad*) God the everlasting Refuge; God the self-sufficient Master. God the Resistance! (سورة الإخلاص, *Sūrat al-Ikhlas* 112:2) A massacre set to melody, genocide disguised as children's verse, memory erased in meter and rhyme:

> *"In 1492, Columbus sailed the ocean blue."*[13]

---

[12] From the triliteral root ص-م-د (*ṣād-mīm-dāl*), which in classical Arabic denotes steadfastness, firmness, and the act of remaining unmoved or resisting collapse under strain. In Qur'anic usage, the root appears in al-Ṣamad (Qur'an 112:2), a divine epithet meaning "the Everlasting Refuge" or "the one upon whom all depend," underscoring absolute stability and reliability. In a Pauline framework, this semantic field resonates not only with exhortations to "stand firm" (στήκετε, *stēkete*, e.g., Galatians 5:1; Philippians 4:1) but also with the function of ὑπομονή (*hypomonē*), endurance with patience under sustained pressure (cf. Romans 5:3-4; James 1:3-4), until the appointed time of God's triumph over the powers of tyranny (cf. 1 Corinthians 15:24-28). Thus, the root bridges Qur'anic and Pauline idioms of endurance, combining unyielding stability with the patient perseverance that defines steadfast resistance. See Lane, Edward William, *An Arabic-English Lexicon, Book I,* Williams and Norgate, 1863, p. 1726-1727; Liddell, Henry George, and Robert Scott, *A Greek-English Lexicon,* 7th ed., p. 845; and Bauer, Walter, et al., *A Greek-English Lexicon of the New Testament and Other Early Christian Literature,* 4th ed., University of Chicago Press, 2021, pp. 839-840.

[13] Stoner, Winifred Sackville, Jr. "The History of the United States." Facts in Jingles, Bobbs-Merrill, 1915. This jingle opens

Together, the three Abrahamic scrolls challenge blasphemous systems that claim to represent the will of the Most High while erasing the particularity of his creation, as Paul Nadim Tarazi proclaims in *The Rise of Scripture*, the *toledot* of the Heavens and the Earth:

> *"The heavens tell of the glory of God; And their expanse declares the work of his hands." (Psalm 19:1)*

So too, the triliteral root.

Today, as the children of empire continue to draw borders and rename languages, the heirs of al-Andalus and the Levant recover the legacy of shared study. We return to the root: to the consonant, to the verb, to the Command of God. We refuse the ideologies that would bind us in the chains of modern iterations of the Trastámaran lie.[14] To Columbus and his children, we say:

---

with the well-known couplet "In fourteen hundred ninety-two, Columbus sailed the ocean blue, and found this land, land of the Free, Beloved by you, beloved by me…" which was already in print by 1892 as a schoolroom mnemonic commemorating the 400th anniversary of Columbus's first voyage, though its original author remains unknown. The rhyme continues to be taught to schoolchildren in the United States today.

[14] Isabella I of Castile and Ferdinand II of Aragon, both of the Trastámara dynasty, a royal house originating in the County of Trastámara in Galicia, married in 1469, uniting the crowns of Castile and Aragon and laying the groundwork for Spain's political unification. As Trastámara monarchs, they oversaw the Reconquista's completion with Granada's conquest in 1492, enacted the Alhambra Decree expelling Jews, and sponsored Columbus's first voyage. See Henry Kamen, *The Spanish Inquisition: A Historical Revision,* 4th ed., Yale University Press, 2014, pp. 88-92;

> *"Woe to him who gets evil gain for his house, to set his nest on high, to be safe from the reach of harm! You have devised shame for your house by cutting off many peoples; you have forfeited your life. For the stone will cry out from the wall, and the beam from the woodwork respond." (Habakkuk 2:9-11)*

لا إلهَ إلا وَاحِدٌ (*lā ilāha illā wāḥidun*) There is no God but one. (1 Corinthians 8:4) Praise belongs to him alone, "the proprietor of every blessing, the fulfiller of every desire, the bestower of every request, the completer of every petition, the hearer of every supplication, and the one who brings every hope to completion."[15]

At his Command, let the sons of Noah meet at the oasis, beneath the sheltering palm tree, defying the settler identities carved into our flesh since 1492:

> *"O Lord, I have heard the report of you, and your work, O Lord, do I fear. In the midst of the years revive it; in the midst of the years make it known; in wrath, O Lord, remember mercy." (Habakkuk 3:2)*

---

and Peggy K. Liss, *Isabel the Queen: Life and Times,* Oxford University Press, 1992, pp. 156-160.

[15] Jonah Ibn Janāḥ. *Kitāb al-Uṣūl*, edited by Adolf Neubauer, Oxford, Clarendon Press, 1875, p. 91.

Rise, Andalus

Our street
does not belong to Isabel.
We do not answer to Congress.

Columbus is not from us,
and he does not beget us.

We do not know Clinton,
Cesar Chavez is our brother.

From the gate of Alif
to the gate of Yā',

Rise, Andalus. Rise!

A voice cries out
in the wilderness:
"Make straight his path!"

He is our Shepherd.

For Noah had not two,
but three sons.
And we are brothers.

Come.
Gather with us
under the palm tree.

Rise, Andalus. Rise!

'Ulamā' al-Andalus[16]

Contemporary Islamic scholars describe medieval al-Andalus, where Muslims, Christians, and Jews developed a shared grammatical methodology, largely unhindered by theology or identity, as a model of التعايش (*al-ta'āyush*, "coexistence") or العيش المشترك (*al-'aysh al-mushtarak*, "shared living"). Drawing on the triliteral root analysis pioneered by the scholars of al-Andalus, and beginning with the function of ἐρῆμος (*eremos*), this book demonstrates how Luke's Gospel employs terminology that activates a core Semitic vocabulary resisting human imperial pretension across Hebrew, Arabic, and Greek scriptures, ultimately disclosing that the so-called war on terror is, in truth, a centuries-old war on the Gospel of Jesus Christ.

Emperor Justinian stands as a striking example of this imperial harlotry, filtering Scripture through political agenda, a pattern that continues in contemporary discourse where settled elites twist biblical texts to justify the very actions Scripture condemns. Justinian's reign, marked by the catastrophic North African campaign against the Vandals, the ruinous Gothic Wars in Italy, and the devastating Justinianic Plague, represents the tragic consequences of imperial ambition masquerading as divine mandate.[17] His translation of Roman law into

---

[16] *'Ulamā' al-Andalus* (عُلَماء الأندلس), literally, "the scholars of al-Andalus." The term designates the Jewish, Christian, and Muslim learned figures of medieval Iberia.

[17] For Justinian's North African campaign, the Gothic Wars, the Justinianic Plague, and his codification of Roman law, see J. A. S. Evans, *The Age of Justinian: The Circumstances of Imperial Power* (Routledge, 2000), and Peter Sarris, *Justinian and the Later Roman Empire* (Cambridge UP, 2014).

Greek directly contradicts the biblical witness that rejects both Roman jurisprudence and Greek intellectual tradition.

These campaigns were catastrophically expensive, devastating to local populations, and, like all imperial games, ended in failure. Together with the Justinianic Plague, a lethal epidemic that ravaged both population and economy, these calamities fractured the region's future. Though the Western Empire had already collapsed in the fifth century, Justinian's ambitions destabilized its successors and hindered the organic development of local societies.[18] We might have avoided the first Dark Age—or at least, the first one we know of—had Justinian not tried to impose a new civilization atop the ruins of the old.

As I explained in *Dark Sayings,* Justinian outdid Solomon—and now Netanyahu—accomplishing in one week what a democratic American proxy could not achieve in the first year of his campaign through direct genocidal violence. Both represent manifestations of imperial harlotry: the systematic co-optation of biblical language to justify the very actions Scripture condemns. As God's messenger, Paul, said, "there is no God but one," the heavenly Shepherd who claims no embassy, joins no assembly, and takes no seat at human councils. He casts no vote, answers to no electorate, and has no

---

[18] For the destructive costs of Justinian's military campaigns, the devastation of the Justinianic Plague, and their destabilizing impact on Mediterranean societies, see Peter Heather, *Rome Resurgent: War and Empire in the Age of Justinian* (Oxford UP, 2018); Mischa Meier, *Justinian: Emperor, Soldier, Saint* (Oxford UP, 2023); and Lester K. Little, ed., *Plague and the End of Antiquity: The Pandemic of 541-750* (Cambridge UP, 2007).

constituents. His throne is in the heavens, far beyond human reach, where maps are not drawn.

As such, this analysis demonstrates how Luke's story of the Gerasene demoniac functions as a deliberate assault on the foundational structures of Greco-Roman imperialism, utilizing precise linguistic correspondences that reveal the text's insurgent character when examined in its original linguistic context.

Methodological Considerations: Translation and Function

The English rendering of biblical texts often obscures rather than illuminates scriptural function. Terms like "lonely place" or "desolate place" for the Greek ἐρῆμος *(eremos)* represent interpretive disasters that reduce complex biblical usages to psychological categories susceptible to contemporary manipulation. The Bible in English cannot serve as the words of God; translation functions only as an aggregative syntax machine, similar to large language models, where patterns emerge through repetition rather than through individual semantic units.

Meaning itself operates as the mechanism of Trastámaran propaganda. When we "engage" with English translations, we begin from an interpretive void, discussing phantoms rather than textual artifacts. The marketing apparatus of empire manufactures psychological crises. For example, articles in the New York Times about loneliness epidemics designed to draw readers into dependence on the very systems that "shut them out" of the kingdom. (Galatians 4:17) They manufacture services and products to amplify the epidemics they market, the vicious circle that Paul warns against in Galatians.

Only by examining original linguistic functions can we approach what the biblical authors *actually* constructed. What we do with these correspondences constitutes interpretation, yes, but the correspondences themselves represent discoverable phenomena that cannot be debated. They exist as textual facts. An English function has no value scripturally, but in aggregate, taken as a whole, translations convey patterns. Yet individual terms like "desert," "lonely place," or "wilderness" provide no help in New Testament interpretation. We must examine what these terms correspond to in the original text to have any chance of hearing what the author has accomplished.

Linguistic Analysis: *eremos* and Its Hebrew Correspondence

The Greek verb ἐρημόω *(eremoo)*, meaning to dry up, make desolate, destroy, or lay waste, corresponds to the Hebrew triliteral root ב-ר-ח (*ḥet-reš-bet*). In its Old Testament usage, this function specifically refers to the desolation or destruction of lands, cities, and nations, the systematic undoing of human structures, particularly in the context of divine judgment.

This correspondence appears throughout both Hebrew and Arabic textual traditions, signifying civilizational collapse as the consequence of injustice, human arrogance, or rejection of divine instruction. The function operates not randomly but as the inevitable result of resistance to God's covenant. In both Hebrew and Arabic, it signifies the undoing not only of cities but of structures and human systems, especially in the wake of divine judgment.

Significantly, this triliteral root also designates Mount Ḥoreb, the site of divine lawgiving. The same linguistic function that describes destruction and desolation also names the location where God establishes his covenant. This connection cannot be coincidental. It represents the fundamental tension between divine and human systems of order. The same triliteral appears as both the site where divine law is given and the agent of God's judgment against human rebellion.

Septuagint Correspondences: Archeological Excavation

The lexical correspondence between Greek ἐρημόω (*eremoo*) and Hebrew ב-ר-ח (*ḥet-reš-bet*) appears throughout the Septuagint in contexts that consistently demonstrate divine opposition to human imperial structures. These passages reveal distinct thematic patterns that illuminate Luke's deployment of the term.

Divine Judgment Against Nations and Cities

- **Isaiah 37:18**: "Truly, O Lord, the kings of Assyria have laid waste (*ḥet-reš-bet / eremoo*) all the nations and their lands." Here the root describes imperial devastation, but significantly, it appears in Hezekiah's prayer acknowledging God's sovereignty over even Assyrian conquest. The text subjugates human imperial power to divine authority.
- **Ezekiel 26:2, 19**: The prophecy against Tyre employs the root twice, describing both the city's pride in Jerusalem's fall and its own coming

desolation. "I will make you a desolate (*ḥet-reš-bet / eremoo*) city, like cities that are not inhabited." This demonstrates the principle that imperial powers who celebrate others' destruction become subject to the same divine judgment.

- **Ezekiel 29:12; 30:7**: Against Egypt, the root appears in contexts of comparative desolation. Egypt will be "desolate among desolated countries" and "waste among wasted cities." The repetitive structure emphasizes that no imperial system escapes this pattern of divine judgment.

Natural Destruction

- **Isaiah 44:27**: "Who says to the deep, 'Be dry (*ḥet-reš-bet / eremoo*), I will dry up your rivers.'" This passage explicitly connects natural phenomena with divine command, demonstrating that the same power that controls natural forces opposes human pretension.
- **Isaiah 51:10**: "Was it not you who dried up (*ḥet-reš-bet / eremoo*) the sea, the waters of the great deep; who made the depths of the sea a way for the redeemed to cross over?" The Exodus reference establishes the paradigmatic use of this function; divine power exercised against kingly systems (Egypt).
- **Job 14:11**: "As waters fail from the sea, and a river wastes away and dries up (*ḥet-reš-bet / eremoo*), so mortals lie down and do not rise again." Here, the root appears within the framework of wisdom literature, but Job speaks not with reverence, but with a tone of arrogance that borders on blasphemy, inviting divine wrath. His analogy between human

mortality and inevitable natural cycles (e.g., the drying up of rivers and lakes) reflects a misunderstanding: these processes are not autonomous or fated; they are subject to divine command. This is precisely what the semantic itinerary of the root ב-ר-ח (*ḥet-reš-bet*) indicates to the trained ear. Job's lament assumes that desolation חורב (*ḥoreb*), and death flow from the fixed laws of nature, yet Scripture consistently portrays such outcomes as the consequence of disobedience, not passive natural cycles. Job fails to uphold the foundation of wisdom: that God alone gives and takes away, governs waters and wilderness, and commands both life and its end.

Self-Inflicted Imperial Ruin

- **Isaiah 49:17**: "Your destroyers (*ḥet-reš-bet / eremoo*), and those who laid you waste go away from you." This paradox exposes the inherent futility of imperial grandeur: the very agents who construct and elevate a civilization are the same instruments through which its undoing is assured. The function ב-ר-ח (*ḥet-reš-bet*) evokes both physical devastation, both a lament and a warning.

Indeed, Justinian's ambitious building projects, monuments to Roman authority, pit him against the Suffering Slave of Second Isaiah. Drawn in blood, his undertakings strained imperial resources, overextended military campaigns, and exacerbated internal fragility. The emperor's architects, in outdoing the Bible's villains and his enemies, unwittingly advanced its own failure.

'Ulamā' al-Andalus

- **Ezekiel 26:2**: Tyre's celebration of Jerusalem's fall: "Aha, broken is the gateway of the peoples; it has swung open to me; I shall be replenished, now that it is waste *(ḥet-reš-bet / eremoo)*" immediately precedes the prophecy of Tyre's own desolation. Imperial powers that profit from others' destruction ensure their own ruin. Here, we witness a moment of imperial gloating that triggers divine judgment. Human arrogance becomes the catalyst for God's pronouncement of Tyre's own downfall in the verses that follow.

Military and Juridical Contexts

- **Judges 16:24**: The Philistines praise their god Dagon: "Our god has given Samson our enemy into our hand, the ravager *(ḥet-reš-bet / eremoo)* of our country." This passage demonstrates how the root operates in contexts of military conflict where kingly powers attribute their temporary success to false gods, again, arrogance is their undoing. Like Tyre and Babylon, the Philistines misread power, failing to perceive the hidden hand of the biblical God, who alone governs ruin and restoration.
- **Amos 7:9**: "The high places of Isaac shall be made desolate (*ḥet-reš-bet /eremoo*), and the sanctuaries of Israel shall be laid waste; and I will rise against the house of Jeroboam with the sword (*ḥereb*)." The prophecy connects religious sites with political structures and notably employs both the verbal form ח-ר-ב (*ḥet-reš-bet* as "make desolate") and the nominal form (*ḥereb* as "sword") in the same verse, calling to mind the alignment of Torah and destruction in

Exodus and demonstrating the functional unity of the triliteral root.

Restoration Through Destruction

- **Isaiah 60:12**: "For the nation and kingdom that will not serve you shall perish; those nations shall be utterly laid waste (*ḥet-reš-bet / eremoo*)." This passage appears in a restoration oracle, indicating that the destruction of imperial systems serves the ultimate purpose of establishing divine reign. A reminder that refusal to submit to divine rule results in desolation, reinforcing the larger prophetic threat that all political power must be subordinated to God's literary kingdom.
- **Jeremiah 33:9**: In a restoration context, the root appears in describing how Jerusalem's restoration will cause fear among nations: "And this city shall be to me a name of joy, a praise and a glory before all the nations of the earth who shall hear of all the good that I do for them; they shall fear and tremble because of all the good and all the prosperity I provide for it." The implied contrast with previous desolation ח-ר-ב (*ḥet-reš-bet*) demonstrates the pattern of divine judgment followed by restoration.

Thematic Synthesis

These Septuagint correspondences reveal consistent patterns that support the interpretation of Luke 8:30. The Hebrew triliteral ח-ר-ב (*ḥet-reš-bet*) and its Greek equivalent ἐρημόω (*eremoo*) systematically describe:

1. **Divine opposition to imperial or kingly pride**: Assyria, Babylon, Tyre, and Egypt all encounter this judgment.
2. **Divine authority undergirding political judgment**: Natural forces demonstrate divine power over human systems (Isaiah 44:27; 51:10; Job 14:1)
3. **Self-destructive nature of imperial systems**: Powers that destroy others ensure their own ruin. (Isaiah 49:17; Ezekiel 26:2; Qur'an, Sūrat al-Ḥashr سورة الحشر "The Exile" or "The Gathering" 59:2: "They destroy their houses with their own hands.") The Banū Naḍīr (بَنُو النَّضِير) tribe,[19] discussed below, demolishing their own fortresses during exile, representing self-inflicted civilizational collapse.
4. **Juridical dimension**: The root connects with legal/covenantal contexts. Exodus 32:27: Moses commands the Levites at Ḥoreb to take up their swords חֶרֶב (*ḥereb*) and execute judgment within the camp because of the golden calf incident.
5. **Restorative purpose**: Destruction serves the establishment of divine reign (e.g. Jeremiah 33:9)

---

[19] "It is he who expelled the ones who disbelieved among the people of the book from their homes at the first gathering. You did not think they would go out, and they thought their fortresses would protect them from God. But God came upon them from where they had not expected..." (Qur'an, Sūrat al-Ḥashr سورة الحشر "The Exile" or "The Gathering" 59:2-5) الحشر (*al-Ḥashr*) refers to the gathering or exile, specifically relating to the expulsion of the Jewish tribe Banū Naḍīr from Medina. The word also carries the function of resurrection or the final gathering on the Day of Judgment.

Comparative Semitic Analysis: Arabic Cognates and Qur'anic Itinerary

The broader Semitic linguistic context reinforces this interpretation through parallel Arabic roots that share the same triliteral pattern and function. Two distinct but related Arabic roots illuminate the Hebrew correspondence and demonstrate the cross-linguistic consistency of these concepts across Semitic Scripture.

Root 1: خ-ر-ب (khā'-rā'-bā'): *Destruction and Desolation*

The Arabic triliteral root خ-ر-ب *(khā'-rā'-bā')* carries the core function of destruction, ruin, and desolation. In Qur'anic usage, it appears in Form IV as يُخْرِبُونَ *(yukh'ribūna)* in Qur'an, Sūrat al-Ḥashr سورة الحشر "The Exile" or "The Gathering" 59:2: "They destroy يُخْرِبُونَ *(yukh'ribūna)* their houses with their own hands and the hands of the believers."

This passage describes the Banū Naḍīr (بَنُو النَّضِير) tribe tribe demolishing their own fortresses during their exile from Medina. In Qur'anic terms, Banū Naḍīr reflects a recurring pattern: the community with scriptural knowledge أهل الكتاب *(ahl al-kitāb,* "people of the book") that chooses institutional preservation over submission to God's words when confronted with prophetic authority. This represents a paradigmatic example of how institutions possessing scriptural knowledge destroy themselves when they prioritize institutional survival over divine instruction. The Qur'anic text emphasizes that destruction results not from external force but from the internal contradiction of claiming scriptural authority while resisting prophetic utterence.

This theme parallels the Qur'anic critique of other institutional powers—tribal, familial, or economic—that resist prophetic authority, following the consistent line of critique against imperial institutions that invoke divine sanction while rejecting divine content.

The thematic significance parallels the Hebrew usage: ruin emerges as the inevitable consequence of rejecting divine instruction, and this destruction often manifests as self-inflicted collapse rather than external conquest.

Root 2: ح-ر-ب (ḥā'-rā'-bā') - *War and Divine Opposition*

The Arabic root ح-ر-ب *(ḥā'-rā'-bā')* designates war, enmity, and conflict, but specifically in contexts of opposition to divine order. In Form III, يُحَارِبُونَ (*yuḥāribūna*) appears in Qur'an, al-Mā'idah المائدة "The Table Spread" 5:33:

> *"The recompense of those who wage war against God and his Apostle and spread corruption on earth is only that they shall be killed or crucified or their hands and feet be cut off from opposite sides, or they be exiled from the land."*

This passage describes not ordinary warfare but extreme aggression against divine instruction: rebellion, terror, and systematic lawlessness. The prescribed punishments (execution, crucifixion, exile) represent divine justice responding to fundamental challenges to God's authority.

The "war" referenced by this root transcends military conflict to signify comprehensive hostility to divine instruction. The divine response involves purification through justice that removes sources of corruption from the community, reminiscent of Deuteronomy.

Coparative Triliteral Analysis

- The Arabic triliteral root خ-ر-ب (*khāʾ-rāʾ-bāʾ*) carries the core function of ruin or desolation. In Qur'an 59:2, it is used to describe the self-destruction of Banū Naḍīr, conveying the idea that arrogance leads to the collapse of civilizations.
- The Arabic triliteral root ح-ر-ب (*ḥāʾ-rāʾ-bāʾ*) functions as war or hostility. In Qur'an 5:33, it appears in the context of divine justice against rebellion, expressing how divine law purifies through judgment.
- The Hebrew triliteral root ח-ר-ב (*ḥet-reš-bet*) functions as sword, desolation, and refers to Ḥoreb. In Exodus 32:27, the sword's judgment at the site of lawgiving, intertwining law and violent purification.

Textual Synthesis

Both Arabic roots خ-ر-ب (*khāʾ-rāʾ-bāʾ*, "ruin") and ح-ر-ب (*ḥāʾ-rāʾ-bāʾ*, "war") function in Qur'anic discourse as instruments of divine correction that parallel the Hebrew triliteral ח-ר-ב (*ḥet-reš-bet*). The pattern demonstrates consistent Semitic lexical vocabulary:

1. **Rejection of divine teaching produces ruin** خ-ر-ب: Communities that abandon divine instruction create the conditions for their own collapse.
2. **Violent rebellion invokes purifying judgment** (ח-ר-ב/ح-ر-ب): Systematic opposition

to divine authority invites divine intervention and justice

3. **Destruction serves restoration**: In both Qur'anic and Biblical traditions, the dismantling of corrupt human systems clears space for reasserting divine instruction.

The Method of al-Andalus

Intertextual Excavation Through Triliteral Root Systems

The triliteral Semitic root system functions as the deep connective tissue among Hebrew, Arabic and the extant Semitic languages that gave rise to the divine language of the anti-Hellenic scriptures, and thus among the Old and New Testaments (via LXX lexicographical study), and the Qur'an. When ἔρημος *(eremos)* in the Greek New Testament is understood not as a merely "Greek" word, but as a semantic rendering of Semitic triliteral roots, we undertake the precise work of intertextual excavation that was central to the school of al-Andalus.

This Judaeo-Arabic methodology developed systematically through key scholars. Yehuda Ḥayyūj (يهوذا الحيّوج, c. 945-1000), was the first to emphasize the significance of triliteral roots in Hebrew, laying the groundwork for future scholarship.[20] Youna Ibn Janāḥ (يونه ابن جناح, c. 990-1050) then fully systematized and documented this concept, establishing foundational

[20] Martínez Delgado, José. "Ḥayyūj, Judah (Abū Zakariyyā Yaḥyā) ben David al-Fāsi." *Encyclopedia of Jews in the Islamic World,* edited by Norman A. Stillman, Brill, 2010.

Hebrew grammar and triliteral root lexicography in his *Kitāb al-Uṣūl* (كتاب الأصول, *The Book of Roots*), producing a definitive methodology that shaped both Biblical and Qur'anic linguistic scholarship.[21] Mousa ibn Chiquitilla (موسى ابن شقيطلة, c. 1020-1080) advanced Hebrew lexicography and triliteral root analysis;[22] Ishaq ibn Barūn (إسحاق ابن برون, c. 1035-1135) developed systematic Hebrew-Arabic comparative philology in his *Kitāb al-Muwāzana* (كتاب الموازنة, *The Book of Comparison*);[23] Ibrahim ibn 'Ezra (1167-1089, إبراهيم ابن عزرا) applied triliteral root analysis to biblical commentary;[24] and Yehuda ibn Tibbun (يهودا ابن تبون, c. 1120-1190)

---

[21] Webster, Blaise. *It Only Takes One Word: The Necessity of Strict Lexicography in the Study of Biblical Literature.* Journal of the Orthodox Center for the Advancement of Biblical Studies, vol. 13, no. 1, 2024, pp. 4-5.

[22] Isaac, Daniel Elan Menahem. "Adopción del triliteralismo entre los exegetas ibéricos, aceptación y rechazo: el caso de Moisés ibn Chiquitilla." *Sefarad*, vol. 83, no. 2, 2023, p. 237. *"I reach the conclusion that among the circles of grammarians in Saragossa in the 11th and 12th centuries, Ibn Chiquitilla tends towards the opinions of Judah Ḥayyūj, accepting the theoretical underpinnings of his system of grammar and rejecting any exception to the triradical roots, including the biradicalism of Ibn Nağrela and Ibn 'Ezra."*

[23] "Ibn Barun, Abu Ibrahim Isḥaq." Jewish Encyclopedia. *"Ibn Barun was well versed in Arabic literature and was the first to realize the close connection existing between Hebrew grammatical and lexicographical forms and those of the Arabic. This connection was pointed out by him in a work entitled Kitāb al-Muwāzana, divided into two parts, the first treating of Hebrew grammar in comparison with Arabic, the second of lexicography."*

[24] Sáenz-Badillos, Ángel. *A History of the Hebrew Language.* Cambridge: Cambridge University Press, 1993. pp. 203-206

contributed through translation and lexicography as the "father of Hebrew translators."[25]

This progression demonstrates how scholarship in this period moved from basic Semitic triliteral analysis (Ibn Janāḥ) through comparative Semitic philology (Ibn Barūn) to applied biblical interpretation (Ibn 'Ezra)—precisely the methodological sequence that this analysis of Luke's ἔρημος *(eremos)* follows. Contemporary figures from West Asia, such as Kamal Salibi, Skandar Abou Chaar, [26] and Paul Nadim Tarazi, continue this tradition,[27] against the grain of Crusader, Orientalist and Trastámaran propaganda in Western scholarship. Notably, following the line of Ibn Janāḥ, Tarazi, writing

---

[25] Weinberg, Joanna. "Ibn Tibbon, Judah." *Encyclopedia of Jews in the Islamic World*, edited by Norman A. Stillman, Brill, 2010.

[26] Iskandar Abou-Chaar argues that Arabic roots are essential for understanding key names and terms in *Rereading Isaiah 40–55: As the Project Launcher for the Books of the Law and the Prophets* (St. Paul, MN: OCABS Press, 2021). He insists that names such as Abraham and Israel are best explained from Arabic rather than Hebrew. Thus, Abraham (*'abraham)* combines *'ab* ("father") with ر-ح-م *(rā'-ḥā'-mīm)*, which in Arabic yields usages such as "emaciated sheep," "ointment," and "light drizzle," clarifying the Slave's role (pp. 42-43). Likewise, Israel is derived not from Hebrew *śrh* ("strive") but from Arabic ي-س-ر *(yā'-sīn-rā'),* "ease, prosperity," casting Jacob as one seeking "easy street" (pp. 56-57). Abou-Chaar further shows that the Hebrew root ברא (*br',* "create") resonates with the Arabic ب-ر-أ (*bā'-rā'-hamza,* "to free, to make pure"), and the Hebrew ברר (*bet-reš-'alef,* "to purify") with Arabic ب-ر-ر (*bā'-rā'-rā',* "uprightness, sonship") (pp. 26-27). Arabic, he explains, provides the primary key to the names and wordplays that structure Isaiah 40-55 and its role as the project launcher for the Law and the Prophets.

[27] Webster, Blaise. *It Only Takes One Word: The Necessity of Strict Lexicography in the Study of Biblical Literature.* Journal of the Orthodox Center for the Advancement of Biblical Studies, vol. 13, no. 1, 2024, pp. 6-9.

in English, emphasizes specific lexicographic terms like الأصل (*al-aṣl*, "the root") and اللفظ (*al-lafẓ*, "the utterance"), highlighting systematic logic and triliteral function in prophetic and Semitic texts.

Reclaiming eremos *Through Multiple Semitic Correspondences*

The Greek ἔρημος *(eremos)* translates several distinct Hebrew roots, each activating different semantic fields within the shared Semitic textual vocabulary:

1. מ-ד-ב-ר (*MEM-DALET-BET-REŠ*) *MIDBAR*

Root usage: "to speak" ד-ב-ר (*dalet-bet-reš*) with *mem* prefix indicating location, literally, "place of speaking" or "pasture." Greek ἔρημος (*eremos)* translates מִדְבָּר (*midbār)* more frequently than any other Hebrew term. The Qur'anic inter-function connects to ب-ر-ي (*bāʾ-rāʾ-yāʾ*) "to create" or د-ب-ر (*dāl-bāʾ-rāʾ)* "to manage, arrange", both embedded in prophetic contexts of wilderness as divine testing and command.

מִדְבָּר (*midbār)* designates not barrenness but the location where God speaks, where דִּבֶּר אֱלֹהִים (*dibber ʾelohim*, "divine speech") occurs. ἔρημος *eremos*, therefore, represents not merely "desert" but the theater of the words of God, the space where divine speech interrupts human systems.

2. ש-מ-ם (*ŠIN-MEM-MEM*) *ŠEMAMAH*

Root usage: to be desolate, astonished. ἔρημος *eremos* mirrors this desolation, but the Hebrew carries connotations of shock and horror at witnessing divine judgment. The Arabic echo appears in ص-م-ت (*ṣād-mīm-*

tā') "to be silent", or ش-م-س (*shīn-mīm-sīn*) "sun/desert exposure", lexically different but poetically consonant. In Qur'anic usage, desolate land becomes a sign آية (*āyah*) of divine punishment or renewal. The term *āyah,* meaning both "verse" and "sign", corresponds to the Hebrew אותות (*'otot*) "signs", establishing the textual principle that natural phenomena function as divine will, and conversely, that the text itself is the sign, since the verse contains God's action, a concept that extends into Shia religious terminology, where the designation, آية الله, (*āyatullāh*) indicates the one assigned to interpret divine signs.

3. ע-ר-ב (*'AYIN-REŠ-BET*) *'ĂRABAH*

Root usage: The Hebrew root ע-ר-ב (*'ayin-reš-bet*) conveys a rich semantic field encompassing "to mix," "to set (as in evening)," and "desert." This triliteral root shares linguistic heritage with the Arabic root ع-ر-ب (*'ayn-rā'-bā')*. For example, الأعراب (*al-a'rāb*) in Qur'an, Sūrat al-Tawbah سورة التوبة "The Repentance" 9:97 refers to the Bedouin, those living outside the collective, often portrayed as culturally raw or resistant to the call of the مُؤَذِّن (*mu'adhdhin*). At the same time, the term عَرَبي (*'arabī)* can refer to eloquence and the purity of the Arabic language (e.g., Qur'an 16:103, 26:195), establishing a tension between self-referential vs. text-referential nomadic pastoralism.

The עֲרָבָה *('arabah)* a geographic region in the Hebrew text (stretching south from the Dead Sea) intersects with this semantic network, linking the wilderness as a liminal space of both divine testing and cultural cross-pollination. In this framework, the desert becomes a contested space of identity, where divine instruction, mixing of peoples, and prophetic encounter all take shape, mirrored in both Biblical and Qur'anic traditions.

4. י-שׁ-ם (*YOD-ŠIN-MEM*) *YEŠIMON*

Root usage: poetic barrenness, emphasizing uninhabitable terrain. Arabic correspondence: س-م-م (*sīn-mīm-mīm*) "to poison" or "to desiccate," capturing the spiritual danger and sterility. In Qur'anic discourse, scorching wind and barren land motifs evoke God's judgment:

1. *"In scorching wind* سَمُومٍ (samūm*) and boiling water, and in the shade of black smoke, neither cool nor beneficial." (Qur'an,* Sūrat al-Wāqiʿah سورة الواقعة *"The Inevitable" or "The Great Event" 56:42-44)*

2. *"And the jinn we created before from a scorching fire of wind* نَّارِ ٱلسَّمُومِ (nār as-samūm*)." (Qur'an, Sūrat al-Ḥijr* سورة الحجر *"The Rocky Tract" 15:2*)

3. *"They are but names you have named* إِنْ هِيَ إِلَّا أَسْمَاءٌ سَمَّيْتُمُوهَا (in hiya illā asmā'un sammaytumūhā*), you and your fathers, for which God has sent down no authority." (Qur'an,* Sūrat an-Najm سورة النجم *"The Star" 53:23)*

Echoing 1 Corinthians, the last verse critiques the act of assigning names to false gods or idols, emphasizing that such names are human inventions without divine sanction. The verb سَمَّيْتُمُوهَا (*sammaytumūhā*) is a clear instance of the root س-م-م (*sīn-mīm-mīm*) in its Form II pattern, meaning "to name" or "to designate." The triliteral root thus encompasses physical sterility (*samūm*), spiritual danger (*nār as-samūm*), and false authority (*sammaytumūhā*). All are unified under the concept of corruption that manifests as environmental, spiritual, and institutional barrenness.

The Scholarly Framework of *al-Andalus*

Al-Andalus, particularly in Jewish and Muslim philology, maintained that Scripture must be studied consonantally and inter-lingually, with roots, not translations,[28] as the true vectors of hearing. For our purpose, this methodological insight enables textual discourse across Hebrew מִדְבָּר,חֹרֵב (*midbar, ḥoreb*), Greek ἐρῆμος (*eremos*), and Arabic خَرِبَ (*khariba*) and حَرِبَ (*ḥariba*).

Each term represents not merely vocabulary but a semantic field shaped by triliteral root logic. When this methodology is applied to the Septuagint (LXX), it

---

[28] In al-Andalus, Judeo-Arabic scholars, following earlier figures such as Saadya Gaon, privileged Hebrew, Arabic, and Greek because of their direct connection to the scriptural traditions. Aramaic also held exegetical significance. Latin remained peripheral until later Christian influence, and there is little evidence that vernacular translations, such as Romance or Berber, were ever taken into account in serious study. See Sarah Stroumsa, *Andalus and Sefarad: On Philosophy and Its History in Islamic Spain* (Princeton UP, 2019); Georges Tamer, "Philosophy in al-Andalus: Jewish and Islamic" in The Cambridge Companion to Medieval Philosophy, ed. A. S. McGrade (Cambridge UP, 2003), pp. 92-111; and Dimitri Gutas, *Greek Thought, Arabic Culture: The Graeco-Arabic Translation Movement in Baghdad and Early Society* (2nd-4th/8th-10th centuries) (Routledge, 1998).

reveals the special connections to Arabic خ-ر-ب *(khāʾ-rāʾ-bāʾ)* and ح-ر-ب *(ḥāʾ-rāʾ-bāʾ)* as well as Hebrew מִדְבָּר *(midbar)*, demonstrating how Greek functions as a bridge that preserves and transmits Semitic triliteral root systems across scriptural traditions. This approach makes visible the shared vocabulary that brings together the children of Abraham under the tent of Scripture, in its own words, "Noah had three sons" (Genesis 6:10) which is what makes the method of al-Andalus so powerful for contemporary scriptural study.

Literary Implications

1. Wilderness as Liminal and Revelatory Space

By connecting ἐρῆμος (*eremos*) to מ-ד-ב-ר (*mem-dalet-bet-reš*), the wilderness emerges not as location but as pedagogical space where divine encounter occurs:

- **Moses** in מִדְבָּר *(midbar)* receives divine instruction at Ḥoreb.
- **Jesus** in ἐρῆμος (*eremos*) undergoes testing that establishes his loyalty to his Father's authority. (Matthew 4:1-11, Mark 1:12-13, Luke 4:1-13)
- **Muhammad** in the حراء *(ḥirāʾ)* cave receives divine instruction from the biliteral ح-ر *(ḥāʾ-rāʾ)*.[29]

[29] In Exodus 3:1-2, Moses encounters God for the first time at Ḥoreb, "the mountain of God," where a voice speaks to him from the burning bush. The name Ḥoreb derives from the Hebrew root ח־ר־ב (*ḥet-resh-bet*), meaning "dryness," "desolation," or "ruin" (cf. *Brown–Driver–Briggs Hebrew Lexicon,* s.v. חָרֵב; Gesenius' *Hebrew–Chaldee Lexicon,* s.v. חרב). Ḥoreb, therefore, denotes a remote, arid wilderness, symbolically suited for divine encounter. A parallel

All these represent the same semantic tissue differently instantiated across scriptural traditions. Remarkably, the very place names where Moses and Muhammad

---

emerges with the Qur'anic tradition of the Cave of Ḥirā' (حراء), where the Prophet Muḥammad (مُحَمَّد) received his first revelation in solitude on Jabal al-Nūr (جبل النور), a similarly desolate site. Notably, Ḥirā' is not described with the usual Arabic terms كَهْف (*kahf*, "cave") or جَبَل (*jabal*, "mountain") but retains consonants that echo its biblical antecedent. Though Ḥirā' (حراء) is not etymologically derived from the Hebrew root ח־ר־ב, both names exhibit the consonantal sequence ح-ر-ب (*ḥā'-rā'-bā'*), aside from the Arabic hamza (ء), inviting literary and symbolic comparison. Both sites function as thresholds of wilderness withdrawal for the sake of divine instruction. The Bible implicitly identifies Ḥoreb with Sinai: "When you have brought forth the people out of Egypt, you shall serve God upon this mountain" (Exodus 3:12), establishing Ḥoreb as a canonical place of encounter. In Islamic scholarship, the cave becomes a battleground linked to the same root as مِحْرَاب (*miḥrāb*), the prayer niche, a semicircular recess in the قِبْلَة (*qibla*) "facing" or "confronting" wall where the Imam stands to lead the community. Classical sources such as al-Zamakhsharī (الزمخشري) and al-Rāghib al-Iṣfahānī (الراغب الأصفهاني) connect the *miḥrāb* to the notion of "waging war" against the self. The Arabic root ح-ر-ب (*ḥā'-rā'-bā'*), carries not only the sense of warfare, estrangement, and withdrawal but also, in early usage, the sense of prominence and elevation, denoting the loftiest or most honored space in a dwelling. This sense of height deepens the link to Ḥoreb, the "mountain of God," as both the *miḥrāb* and the mountain function as elevated sanctuaries, set apart, raised above ordinary ground, and chosen as thresholds of divine encounter. In his *al-Risāla al-Qushayriyya*, al-Qushayrī underscores this connection by discussing *khalwa* (retreat/seclusion) as a spiritual discipline, noting the Prophet's practice of withdrawing to Ḥirā' before the first revelation (Knysh, Alexander. trans., *al-Qushayri's Epistle on Sufism: al-Risala al-Qushayriyya, Reading:* Garnet Publishing, 2007). Thus, both Ḥirā' and Ḥoreb stand as sacred thresholds: arid, elevated sanctuaries where prophetic estrangement from civilization and divine encounter converge.

receive divine revelation—Ḥoreb and Ḥirāʾ—share the same Semitic root pattern that consistently expresses divine opposition to imperial systems throughout Hebrew and Arabic scripture. The wilderness becomes not merely pedagogical space, but specifically space marked by the ح-ر/ח-ר root that opposes human imperial pretension, making divine revelation inherently anti-imperial in its linguistic and geographical foundations, and linking the three Semitic prophets.

2. Joining the Scriptural Conversation

Hearing ἐρῆμος (*eremos*) functionally, not as a Greek linguistic island, but as a Semiticized semantic artifact, the New Testament:

1. Hears back to the Old Testament through Septuagint correspondences.
2. Opens forward into Qur'anic discourse through shared triliteral function.
3. Participates in the grammar of divine encounter that al-Andalus scholars recognized as unified scriptural landscape.

This approach reveals how Luke 8:30 shares the literary geography of prophecy: a unified scriptural terrain formed by root, desert, and divine words, where the Scriptural God's authority confronts human imperial pretension across linguistic and cultural boundaries.

The Sword and Divine Law

In Exodus 32:27, the same triliteral ח-ר-ב (*ḥet-reš-bet*) appears as "sword," the instrument of God's judgment.

Moses commands the Levites at Ḥoreb to take up their swords and execute judgment within the camp because of the golden calf incident. This demonstrates how the function operates as both the site of lawgiving and the agent of purifying violence when divine law encounters human rebellion.

The linguistic convergence reveals a biblical principle: this function corresponds consistently with divine wrath directed against human systems that substitute themselves for divine authority. Whether manifested as desolation, sword, or the mountain of lawgiving, the root expresses the collision between divine will and human pretension. This manifestation is expressed in the power of uttering prophetic, and thus, literary, not actual violence.

Legion: The Convergence of Law and Violence

Recent scholarship by Blaise Webster has uncovered the technical precision of Luke's attack on Roman and Greek systems through the term "legion" Λεγιών (*legion*). The Latin *legio*, referring to a Roman military unit of approximately 6,000 soldiers, derives from the Indo-European root meaning "to gather" or "to set in order." From this same root comes *lex* (law)—both terms representing the gathering and ordering that characterizes civilizational control.

Roman legions function as the custodians of *lex*, the instruments of imperial coercion and domination. Law and legion bind together linguistically and ideologically: law enforced through gathered violence. This is the system Jesus confronts in the Decapolis, and Luke identifies it explicitly as demonic.

Notice that throughout the storyline in Luke, Jesus scatters, or is himself rejected. This follows the pattern of the Old Testament. What do people who build churches want to do? They want to gather to themselves. But Jesus scatters to his Father (e.g. Luke 4:33-35, Luke 19:45-46), he does not gather. He scatters so that he can set people free from the city so that they can be gathered to his Father in the wilderness, in the field, שדה (*sadeh*), under the heavens at the end of Matthew's Gospel. His Father is the Shepherd in the heavens whose kingdom rules over all. But what do city builders want to do? The "civilized", whom the children of Herod and Justinian still defend (even in 2025) want to gather in order to control, to set in order. They love to set things in order and tell everybody what to do. In this sense, the best social description of the followers of divine law is "Biblical Anarchist." Human law is, in fact, a farce. All law leads to destruction, as the term Ḥoreb itself suggests. The question is, to what purpose. Divine law destroys to establish justice for the poor, while human law destroys to establish the illusion of control, leading nowhere in the end, as the prophets repeatedly point out, but to the bowels of Sheol.

Lex, derived from λέγω (*lego)*, "to say," "speak," "tell," or "declare," when taken from human lips, represents civilizational control in Scripture, a codified system that enforces order. Roman legions are the custodians of *lex*, the instruments of imperial coercion and domination. One need only observe contemporary events to understand how this functions. *Lex* and legion bind together linguistically and ideologically: law enforced by gathered violence.

Greek Philosophy and the Logos

The Greek λόγος *(logos)* stems from *lego* and represents in Hellenistic philosophy the principle of human reason, logic, and natural law. The results of human reason are evident in our contemporary context. This is why large language models represent a new form of idolatry: they function as sophisticated syntax machines that reflect the human *logos* back to itself, demonstrating the perfection of human narcissism. They gather up human words and put them back in our faces, while serving as tools for social manipulation through technological sophistry. Ironically, these systems also illustrate the absurdity of postmodernism and the possibility that consciousness itself may be a fiction, since they communicate syntactically, competently forgoing abstract meanings.

Conversely, Webster argues, the Pauline appropriation of *logos* constitutes a direct assault on Hellenistic thought.[30] For Paul, *logos* does not designate Greek reason—forget Jordan Peterson and his ilk, frauds promoting the very system Paul opposes—but rather "the word of the cross" ὁ λόγος τοῦ σταυροῦ (*ho logos tou staurou*), foolishness to those who trust in human wisdom but power to those being saved. (1 Corinthians 1:18)

---

30 Webster, Blaise. "In the Beginning was the Logos (of the Cross) — The Crux of Paul and John's Gospel." Blaise Webster, Substack, https:// blaisewebster. substack. com / p/in-the-beginning-was-the-logos-of. Accessed 8 Aug. 2025.

Unlike the constructive Greek *lego*, which seeks order and coherence, the Pauline *lego* operates destructively as an insurgent—dare I say, *anarchic*—word embedded within Greco-Roman structures. It aims at their co-termination through the execution of Jesus, and in this co-termination accomplishes the dismantling of the entire system of Greco-Roman imperialism.

Lex, law, and *lego*, rhetoric and philosophy, represent false structures of control and human meaning that oppose the Pauline Gospel. Jesus, the crucified Messiah, the anointed slave of Second Isaiah—the first מְשֻׁלָּם (*mešullam)*[31]…

> *"Who is blind but my slave [*עַבְדִּי *(*'abdi*)], or so deaf as my messenger whom I send? Who is so blind as he who is at peace with me [*מְשֻׁלָּם *(*mešullam*)], or so blind as the slave of the Lord [*כְּעֶבֶד יְהוָה *(*ke-'ebed yahweh*)?" (Isaiah 42:19)*

…was sent by his Father to destroy human law and human reason, to expose their powerlessness before the Father, who is the only King, our Heavenly Shepherd, in order to raise the poor in place of these human

---

[31] Personal conversation with Blaise Webster, May 22, 2025. The Biblical מְשֻׁלָּם (*mešullam*) and Qur'anic مُسْلِم (*muslim*) are cognates, both derived from the shared Semitic triliteral root ש־ל־מ (*šin-lamed-mem*) in Hebrew and س-ل-م (*sīn-lām-mīm*) in Arabic. The Hebrew participle *mešullam* refers to one who has been made whole, completed, or reconciled, while the Arabic *muslim* denotes one who submits to God and thus is at peace. In both textual traditions, the slave is made whole by submitting; he is at peace because he does not rely on his own sight. Though blind, he sees, because God sees for him, he is not his own reference!

systems of control, so that, as Luke proclaims, the poor would inherit the Kingdom. (Luke 6:20)

The Mission in Decapolis

When Jesus asks the demon "What is your name?" and receives the response "Legion, for many demons had entered him" (Luke 8:30), Luke presents the first military strike in the Slave's mission to dismantle Greco-Roman imperialism. The question represents the moment when the Lukan narrative explicitly identifies the convergence of Roman military power (*legio*), Roman law (*lex*), and Greek philosophy (*logos*) as demonic.

The question of naming carries enormous significance. In the biblical tradition, naming represents authority and recognition. Jesus's demand for the demon's name forces the explicit identification of the enemy: not merely spiritual opposition, but the concrete historical systems of imperial control that masquerade as civilization.

This corresponds precisely to the Qur'anic critique of false naming: "They are but names you have named... for which God has sent down no authority" (53:23). In both traditions, the confrontation with false authority involves exposing the illegitimate nature of human naming. Jesus forces "Legion" to reveal its true identity as a Roman imperial proxy masquerading as legitimate power, while the Qur'an exposes false gods as mere "names you have named" without divine sanction. Both represent the same functional critique: human systems establish apparent authority through naming and linguistic control but lack divine authority.

This connection operates through precise triliteral root correspondences: Hebrew יְשִׁימוֹן (*yešimon*, meaning poetic barrenness and uninhabitable terrain) corresponds to Greek ἐρῆμος (*eremos*) in the Septuagint, which connects to Arabic س-م-م (*sīn-mīm-mīm*) encompassing both sterility سَمُوم (*samūm*) and false naming سَمَّيْتُمُوهَا (*sammaytumūhā*). When Jesus encounters "Legion" in the ἐρῆμος (*eremos*), he confronts false imperial authority in a space linguistically marked by the same root pattern that the Qur'an associates with illegitimate naming. The wilderness becomes the location where divine authority exposes human systems that claim legitimacy through self-designation rather than divine authorization.

This is Jesus's mission when he crosses over into Decapolis: the first strike from the moving caravan of base camp Galilee.[32] This represents what the gospel has been moving toward: the dismantling of Greco-Roman imperialism. All this functions within the name of the demon: Legion.

But the tragic irony of the Gospels, as becomes clear much later in *John's* Gospel, is that *nobody* supports the mission of Jesus. His own people side with Caesar. Everybody wants a human king. This is why our duty requires the relentless perpetuation of the prophetic utterance of the biblical text until the day of the Lord,

---

[32] Cooper, Matthew Franklin, *The Lamb Before Its Shearers* (St. Paul, MN: OCABS Press, 2025), pp. 156-57.

when his work will find its own completion for the sake of the poor, and the avenging of Hind Rajab.[33]

Contemporary Implications

The tragic irony of contemporary discourse lies in the continued defense of "civilization" in the name of the Bible. Political leaders invoke Scripture to justify the very systems the biblical text seeks to destroy. This represents the same imperial harlotry demonstrated by Justinian: the co-optation of biblical language to serve imperial ends while rejecting biblical content.

Netanyahu recently delivered a speech about the Bible and the defense of civilization.[34] He sounds precisely like the leaders of the Gulf States—the tragicomic consequences of colonial Anglo-Saxons having crowned a collection of supposed Bedouin shepherds as kings—men who now sit on their thrones believing in their own manufactured legitimacy. They are the self-referential rebellious Bedouins named in Qur'an 9:97 as الأعراب *(al-*

---

[33] On January 29, 2024, five-year-old Hind Rami Iyad Rajab was trapped in her family's car in Tel al-Hawa, Gaza City, after it was struck by Israeli tank fire that killed six of her relatives. Hind called emergency responders by phone for hours before contact was lost. When rescuers were dispatched, they too were killed. Two weeks later, Hind's body was found in the car, which had been riddled with 335 bullet impacts from Israeli tank fire, according to an investigation by Forensic Architecture. Independent reports confirm Israeli tanks were present at the scene (Forensic Architecture, "The Killing of Hind Rajab"; Al Jazeera, February 12, 2024; The Guardian, February 12, 2024).

[34] Benjamin Netanyahu, *"Statement on Operation Rising Lion and the Defense of Civilization,"* Office of the Prime Minister of Israel, 12 June 2025, www.gov.il/en/departments/news/operation-rising-lion-statement. Accessed July,26, 2025.

aʿrāb): those resistant to the will of the Scriptural God, who alone is عَلِيمٌ حَكِيمٌ (*ʿalīmun ḥakīm*) the "All-Knowing" and "All-Wise." These shepherds, not knowing their limits, live in tension with the أمة (*ummah*) for lack of exposure to the Apostle's teaching:[35]

> *"Indeed, this is your ummah, one ummah* [أ-م-م ('alif-mīm-mīm) *one origin, one leader, one mother, one destination, one* إمام (imām)] *and I am your Lord, so worship me." (Qur'an, Sūrat al-Anbiyā'* سورة الأنبياء *"The Prophets" 21:92)*

In rejection of Luke 8, Justinian, who died in November 565 AD in Constantinople, imposed the monoculture of Roman *lex* upon God's ummah, seeking to crush the authority of his Apostle Paul beneath imperial tyranny; yet only 45 years later, on the Night of Power, Laylat al-Qadr (ليلة القدر), the Night of Fate, in 610, God found Muḥammad in حِرَاء (*ḥīrā'*) and entrusted him with the words of his power. In less than a century, the songbird nestled in the palm tree, singing David's outlawed hymns, as the oudist stirred the great scholars of al-Andalus with the defiant wisdom of Abraham's children, preserved beneath the canopy of

---

35 "مِمَّنْ حَوْلَكُم مِّنَ ٱلْأَعْرَابِ" (*mim-man ḥawlakum mina al-aʿrābi*), "from those around you of the Bedouins," referring to text-referential nomads, who submit to the Prophet's instruction (Qur'an, Sūrah al-Tawbah سورة التوبة "Repentance" 9:101). Contrast with 9:97, where the *aʿrāb* are described as self-referential and "more likely not to know the limits of what God revealed to his Apostle."

empire, enduring like "fire veiled in the reed."[36] Today's elite—East and West—represent a complete inversion, indeed, a betrayal of this Scriptural Power. As God's Messenger, St. Paul, said, prior to Muhammed: لا إِلَٰهَ إِلا هُوَ (*lā ilāha illā hu*) There is no God but him; there is no God but one (1 Corinthians 8:4) and his throne is in the heavens.

It remains tragically comic: defending civilization in the name of the Bible of the Shepherd God, and yet people believe this nonsense. The same pattern repeats across contexts, whether contemporary political leaders invoking biblical authority to justify imperial projects such as Zionism, or public intellectuals like Jordan Peterson promoting Greek philosophical frameworks while claiming biblical grounding, or Gulf State monarchies legitimizing their rule through selective scriptural interpretation enabled by Western imperial systems. If it weren't tragedy, it would be comedy sufficient to warrant sitting with Jonah beneath the vine, popcorn in hand. Contemporary world leaders—كُلُّهُمْ عن آخرهم (*kulluhum ʿan ʾākhirihim*); כֻּלָּם כְּאֶחָד (*kullam keʾeḥad*) "All of them, to the last one; all of them as one."—effectively reenact the sins of the Bible's villains while invoking biblical authority to their own destruction and ours. (cf. Genesis 11:6)

---

[36] The image of "fire in the reed" occurs in the opening verses of Jalāl al-Dīn Rūmī's Masnavī-yi Maʿnavī, known as the "Song of the Reed" (*Nay-nāma*). The reed flute, cut from its reed bed, laments separation from its source, symbolizing the soul's exile from God and its longing for reunion. See Jalāl al-Dīn Rūmī, *The Mathnawí of Jalálu'ddín Rúmí*, translated by Reynold A. Nicholson, vol. 1 (E.J.W. Gibb Memorial, 1926), Book I, lines 1-18.

God save us from the defenders of civilization. They, like church builders, want to gather in order to control, to set in order, to make sure everyone follows their rules. With Isaiah, I sing:

> *"Bring more evils upon them, O Lord; bring more evils upon the glorious ones of the earth." (Isaiah 26:15)*

Conclusion

The linguistic analysis of Luke 8:29-30 reveals a sophisticated critique embedded within precise philological correspondences. The term ἐρῆμος *(eremos)* and its Semitic correlates expose how Luke constructs a systematic dismantling of Greco-Roman imperial structures through its mashal [37] of demonic confrontation.

---

[37] מָשָׁל (*mašal*): A proverb, parable, or riddle, functioning in Scripture as an instrument of judgment once the plain word of the Law is rejected. Moses spoke with God "mouth to mouth," transmitting Torah with unmatched clarity, yet Israel scorned the direct command. Thus Psalm 78 omits Moses and turns instead to parables and riddles חִידוֹת (*ḥidot*). This intensifies in Jeremiah, whose speech grows increasingly enigmatic as his audience hardens, until he himself disobeys his own word and ends in Egypt rather than Babylon. The story of Nathan and David (2 Samuel 12) exemplifies the mashal: rather than accuse David directly, Nathan deploys a parable to ensnare him, exposing guilt under the very Law he dismissed. Jesus, as Ezekiel's "son of man," continues this prophetic mode, introducing parables with "like," so that judgment falls in story form, fulfilling Isaiah's warning: "Lest they should turn and be forgiven" (Isaiah 6, cited in Mark 4). The Septuagint tradition intensifies this trajectory, rendering mashal with Greek terms that emphasize riddles and dark sayings. In ministry, the pattern

This represents more than historical curiosity. The biblical text functions as insurgent literature, designed to expose the powerlessness of human systems before divine authority. The Pauline *logos* operates destructively within imperial structures, not to reform them but to accomplish their termination through the crucified Messiah, God's Suffering Slave.

Our contemporary responsibility involves persistent utterance of these prophetic words until the day of the Lord, maintaining hope in the completion of divine work for the sake of the poor. The biblical text provides not escape from political reality but the vocabulary for its proper interpretation: there is no God but one, whose throne is in the heavens, far beyond the reach of human mapping and control.

The convergence of linguistic evidence across Hebrew, Arabic, and Greek texts demonstrates that Luke 8:29-30 participates in a unified scriptural conversation where divine authority consistently confronts human imperial pretension. Through the Judaeo-Arabic triliteral root methodology of al-Andalus, we observe how the Greek New Testament functions not as Hellenistic, but Semitic literature that participates in inter-functional scriptural discourse with no regard for human institutional boundaries.

The "desolate place" where Legion encounters Jesus represents the space where divine authority dismantles human systems of control: a space that appears

---

endures: one begins with clarity, but when hearers reject the word, the message itself becomes a parable: at once proclamation and entrapment. "He who has ears to hear, let him hear." The rest, "yalla, bye." Paul Nadim Tarazi and Harrison Russin. Psalm 78 Questions. Personal exchange, May 25, 2025.

consistently across scriptural traditions as the location of divine encounter and imperial collapse. In our contemporary context, marked by continued imperial harlotry and the defense of civilization through abuse of biblical language. Inshāʾ Allāh (إن شاء الله), this analysis provides the vocabulary necessary for proper scriptural interpretation and prophetic witness.

Part II

سر في فلاة المرعى

sir fī falāt al-mar‘ā

"Go into the wilderness of pasture"

Human Evil is Not Banal

The Epistemological Catastrophe of Human Self-Deception

It needs only to be spoken: human beings are evil. We are adapted to polish our own image, to excuse our failures, and to weave self-serving tales that soothe our conscience. We denounce hidden horrors even as we exalt the rulers and institutions that commit them. In the season of elections, this duplicity is sanctified beneath the banner of "the lesser of two evils." This is not discernment but the unknowing confession of Scripture's charge against our hypocrisy. Most will never confront their share in the killing fields of Gaza. It is easier to persist in deception, to cradle the Trastámaran lie, than to face the dreadful truth of what we are.

The Triple Constraint of Human Evil

Scripture's exposure of human evil functions under a threefold constraint:

1. **The Natural Mirror**: Not of our making; it reflects reality, not imagination. Our instinct is to look away.
2. **The Manufactured Mirror**: The fairy-tale reflection ("you are the fairest of them all"), artificial mirrors optimized to feed the appetites of monsters.
3. **The Neighbor's Mirror:** The witness of another who sees our behavior, not through the lens of Scripture, but through observation of self-referential conduct in view of self-reference. They

are as blind as we are, but their observation still constrains us.

Of these three, the natural mirror alone is indifferent to vain declarations of honesty or so called "truth-telling." It already knows we are blind, arrogant, and wicked. Its sole purpose is to hold our gaze until we acknowledge what we are in God's eyes.

James and the Natural Face

James 1:23-24 confronts us with the τὸ πρόσωπον τῆς γενέσεως (*to prosopon tes geneseos,* "the natural face" or "the face of birth"). This is not our projection, not the "truth" we speak, but the reality that finds us. No one is truly honest with themselves; we turn from Scripture for no other reason than this: we cannot endure the truth that the human being is the transgression. The prophetic utterance that exposes us invalidates all human self-construction:

- It cannot be developed into self-serving endeavors.
- It cannot be sidestepped.
- It cannot be reversed.
- It does not change.

Religion wrongly amplifies the third constraint as moral virtue. As an institution, it twists Scripture to find fault in others rather than in itself, and in this it mirrors the virtue-signaling of Western politicians and liberal institutions, which perform human morality for applause while evading the mirror of their own hypocrisy. James, however, commands us to look into the natural mirror and not look away.

The Manufactured Meanings vs. Divine Encounter

Human beings are creators of meanings. We construct narratives to avoid the demands of what is *found*: that which has nothing to do with meaning. Meaning, in truth, is a refined form of propaganda. The task is not to "engage" with the gods we create, but to submit to what is there, what is encountered, what is visited upon us, what is found.

The etymology clarifies the distinction. Experience (*ex* + *periri*, "to try, to test") denotes an action that issues from the self. It projects the will and perspective of the subject onto the world, transforming reality into an extension of the ego. Encounter (*in* + *contra*, "into/against") describes an intrusion from outside the self. Something that meets and confronts us on its own terms. One originates in human agency; the other imposes itself as an uninvited judgment. In divine encounter, we become the object of the divine subject.

Experience is self-projection: an idolatrous extension of the ego. Encounter is acquiescence: submission to the judgment that proceeds from divine command. This is the fundamental divide: the Greco-Roman conception of truth as subjective perspective versus the biblical paradigm of revelation as authoritative intrusion.

It is for this reason that one can live through atrocities (with respect to Gaza, perhaps the most horrific of the past century) while continuing daily life as though nothing is amiss. Human beings construct meanings (false gods) to shield themselves from the mirror of Scripture. Turning from the face of their birth, they gaze upon the image fashioned by their own experience.

Human Evil is Not Banal

This methodological gulf between human experience and divine encounter marks the decisive difference between biblical hearing and imperial Christianity, which seeks to impose narrative, meaning, and interpretation, a system of tyranny otherwise and commonly understood as theology. The dominant trajectory of Western scholarship privileges human perspective over divine revelation, reducing scriptural encounter to the banal terms of psychological analysis, the mirage of fools.

The Methodological Framework: Dictionary Writing vs. Imperial Interpretation

As such, contemporary biblical interpretation has fundamentally misunderstood its task. Disciples interacting with Scripture are not called to interpretation but to lexicographical work: the endless writing of dictionaries based on systematic study of word usage across the Semitic textual tradition. This methodology, pioneered by the scholars of al-Andalus, recognizes that hearing emerges not from imposed theological or philosophical systems but from careful attention to how the divine author employs specific terms within original linguistic syntax and itinerary.

In the case of Luke 8:31, the Hebrew נ-ח-ם (*nun-ḥet-mem*) and Arabic ن-ح-م (*nūn-ḥāʾ-mīm*) represent not mere vocabulary items but semantic fields that activate consistent scriptural functions across Hebrew, Arabic, and their Greek correspondences. For example, when Western scholarship attempts to understand biblical consolation apart from this Semitic framework, it inevitably reduces divine encounter to human psychology, missing entirely the text's systematic exposure of imperial allegiances.

I. Triliteral Lexicographical Excavation: παρακαλέω (*parakaleo*) / נ-ח-ם (*nun-ḥet-mem*) / ن-ح-م (*nūn-ḥāʾ-mīm*)

παρεκάλουν αὐτὸν μὴ ἐπιτάξαι αὐτοῖς εἰς τὴν ἄβυσσον ἀπελθεῖν.

"They were imploring him not to command them to go away into the abyss." (Luke 8:31)

Semantic Range and Functional Analysis

The Greek παρακαλέω (*parakaleo*) encompasses encouragement, exhortation, and comfort, corresponding to the Hebrew root נ-ח-ם (*nun-ḥet-mem*), which signifies regret, sorrow, and self-consolation. The Arabic cognate ن-ح-م (*nūn-ḥāʾ-mīm*) maintains parallel semantic usage, indicating the cross-linguistic stability of this triliteral root within the Abrahamic tradition.

When we set aside the presumed "meanings" of words and reject the pseudo-Socratic method, which projects studied confusion (the נָחָשׁ, *naḥash*, of Genesis)[38] in order to lure us away from the divine command, and instead adhere strictly to the text, the first word we encounter is παρακαλέω (*parakaleo*): "they were imploring him."

But this, once again, is our pattern: we fabricate our own meaning—our own propaganda—which is what "meaning" becomes. Thus, when we encounter a word,

---

38 Paul Nadim Tarazi, *The Rise of Scripture* (St. Paul, MN: OCABS Press, 2017) pp. 57-60

even in the Greek New Testament, such as παρακαλέω (*parakaleo*), we have no true sense of what we are hearing, much less of what we are seeing. This term corresponds to נָחַם (*naḥam*) in the canonical consonantal Hebrew text, and in Arabic to the root ن-ح-م (*nūn-ḥāʾ-mīm*). While the Greek term denotes encouragement, its Hebrew counterpart often conveys regret, the sense of sorrow, or worse. And I say "worse" because it can also carry a reflexive force, the hollow act of consoling oneself.

This shift is not a mere semantic curiosity; it is the biblical fault line. To project our own consolations onto the text is to domesticate divine judgment into a mirror of human desire. The dreaded "personal experience," that poisonous legacy of post-Crusader imperial Christianity. To encounter the text, by contrast, is to submit to what is imposed, whether or not it accomodates our preferences.

Divine Regret, Amalek, and the Self-Serving Pleas of the Settled Elite (1 Samuel 15:11, 30)

Scripture teaches not through narrative or meaning, but functionality. In God's Semitic languages, Ephron עפרון (*ʿafaron*) and עפר (*ʿafar*, "dust") share the same root. It is no accident. By this connection, Ephron the Hittite, an outsider, a "dust man", becomes the chosen medium for establishing Hebron, חברון (*ḥebron*), the place of brotherhood, from the triliteral ח־ב־ר (*ḥet-bet-reš*, "to join, unite"). In God's economy, irony abounds: all flesh returns to dust (Genesis 3:19), and it is the "dust man" who provides the burial site where Abraham, Sarah, Isaac, Rebekah, Jacob, and Leah rest in the same אֲדָמָה (*ʾadamah*, "ground, soil, earth, land." Genesis 23:3-20; 49:29-32; 50:13). Hebron is not the property of civilizations; it is the gathering place of dust, the place of brotherhood through death. Like the sacrifice of Isaac, God's command regarding Amalek is a test. By sparing Amalek, Saul denies the scriptural brotherhood of dust. In preserving Agag, he elevates political advantage and self-adoration above obedience to God.

The inheritance underscores this point. Hebron does not fall to Joshua, the military hero, but to Caleb, whose name (כ־ל־ב, *kaf-lamed-bet*, Arabic كَلْب, *kalb*, "dog") marks him as an outsider. The "dog" inherits the place of brotherhood, while the warrior is denied (Joshua 14:13-14). Scripture teaches: God's will is accomplished not through blood, but through outsiders, through the despised, through dust.

This is the pattern betrayed by Saul in 1 Samuel 15. Commanded to annihilate Amalek, Saul spares Agag and seizes the spoils to please his community (1 Samuel 15:1, 4, 9, 15, 21, 24), he listens to the "voice" of the people, turning divine command into self-serving calculation (1 Samuel 15:8-9). Here the same God who once regretted creating humanity now regrets making Saul king:

נִחַמְתִּי כִּי־הִמְלַכְתִּי אֶת־שָׁאוּל לְמֶלֶךְ כִּי־שָׁב מֵאַחֲרַי וְאֶת־דְּבָרַי לֹא הֵקִים

niḥamti ki-himlakti ʾet-shaʾul lemelek ki-shab meʾaḥarai weʾet-debarai lo heqim

*"I regret [*נִחַמְתִּי *(*niḥamti*)] that I have made Saul king because he has turned back from following me and has not carried out my commands." (1 Samuel 15:11)*

Of course, he regretted it. This is what "we" demanded. We asked for a king; we got one (1 Samuel 8:4-7). And kings do what kings always do: they preserve power, build monuments to themselves, and clothe disobedience in the imperial language of piety.

Samuel was incensed and cried out to the Lord all night. Later, in verse 30, Saul, like Legion, makes a self-serving appeal. This is how functionality and itinerary work in the biblical text: Saul seeks to avoid consequence, prioritizing his own standing over obedience to God. In both cases, the plea is not submission but a calculated maneuver to save oneself.

We know the difference. We all recognize the gap between true submission and sycophancy. Between the one who bows to gain an advantage and the one who has accepted their guilt, surrendered to judgment, and ceased bargaining.

Saul's monument at Carmel (1 Samuel 15:12) embodies this rebellion. Instead of honoring God's יד ושם (*yad wa shem*, "a hand and a name," Isaiah 56:5), the principle that creation itself is God's monument, wrought by his hand for his name, Saul exalts his own hand and his own name. Human *yad* builds human *shem*. Saul the king becomes Saul the idolater, usurping divine authorship to establish his own legacy. Sound familiar, Ḥabibi?

The lesson echoes to Ḥebron. When modern leaders claim Ḥebron as their divine inheritance, they repeat Saul's sin. They assert their *yad* (hand, power) to exalt their own *shem* (name, legacy), defiling the very functionality of Scripture. The עפר (*'afar*, "dust") testifies against them: Israelite and Amalekite, conqueror and outsider, all return to the same ground (Ecclesiastes

3:20). Ḥebron is not an emblem of national privilege; it is the place where God gathers dust into brotherhood through death.

Thus, the terminological economy stands: Ephron the "dust man" is God's agent (Genesis 23), Caleb the "dog" is God's heir (Joshua 14), Saul the king is God's rejected (1 Samuel 15), and Hebron the brotherhood is God's possession (Genesis 23; Joshua 14). The divine regret is not weakness; it is the scriptural indictment of every human attempt to establish monuments of blood and soil. All flesh is dust (Genesis 3:19). All names belong to him (Psalm 83:18) and all hands are subject to his hand (Isaiah 41:10).

And what of Amalek?

The Hebrew triliteral ר־א־ש (*reš- ʾalef-šin*) is not a cluster of separate "words." It is one tree with many branches, one root bearing many fruits. *Rešit* (ראשית), *roš* (ראש), *rašut* (רשות), Arabic *raʾīs* (رئيس): all are expressions of the same function: headship.

In Numbers 24:20, the prophet declares: "Amalek was the *rešit* of the nations." Western translators flatten this into "the first," as though the text were counting. But *rešit* does not mean "first" in chronological sequence. It means head, chief, ruler. Amalek was the head of the nations. But as the Apostle said: We know that "there is no God but one." (1 Corinthians 8:4).

And so, Amalek was cast down, and Saul with him. Saul, who sought to withhold from Amalek the brotherhood of the field of Ḥebron. But blessed is he who sets light within praise, whose *shem* is exalted above every name. His will is the straight path, his *shem* is the guide, and his *yad* is over all things.

David's Sentimental Criminality and Contemporary Liberal Rhetoric (2 Samuel 13:39)

David's so-called "consolation" in 2 Samuel bears no relation to repentance. I am weary of apologetic theological devices that attempt to sanitize the brutality of David's reign; psychological constructs such as the "wounded healer." In truth, David resembles a mafia boss who orchestrates atrocities and then retreats into displays of domestic sentimentality. *The Sopranos* provides a vivid analogue: a mob boss who orders killings, then returns home to admire his daughter's elementary school painting, who participates in his nephew's baptism, publicly renouncing Satan three times, and is celebrated for his supposed moral depth. The spectacle is obscene.

And yet, it is the human condition. The prophets expose this reality: we are all, in our own way, sentimental criminals. There is nothing admirable in it. It is simply who we are by nature. This is why mafia dramas are exegetically illuminating. They do not merely entertain; they display, with unflinching accuracy, what James calls "the natural face" in the mirror of Scripture. King David fits this pattern exactly. We are all David. We are all sentimental mobsters.[39]

---

[39] Bakas, Andrea. "David Chase: You may not go on, but the universe goes on and on..." *Vexed*, Episode 30, *Ephesus School Network*, https://feeds.transistor.fm/vexed. It is noteworthy that Bakas gestures toward the prominence of anti-heroes in biblical literature, a point that resonates with the comparison of David to Tony Soprano: both embody the brutal yet sentimental corruption of the human condition, which mafia dramas render with unflinching clarity.

THE GAZA PARADIGM: POLITICAL SELF-CONSOLATION

David's so-called "consolation" in 2 Samuel, functionally identical to the pleading of Legion in Luke 8:31-32, mirrors the rhetorical posture of certain contemporary liberal American politicians who lament the plight of starving children. Such figures employ every term but genocide to avoid legal liability or alienating financial supporters. They craft delicate statements regarding famine in Gaza while simultaneously authorizing arms transfers (parsing the subtle differences between "types" of armaments, God bless them) all the while maintaining food embargoes and suppressing dissent. Even when casting symbolic votes against these measures, they ensure that dissenting voices are removed from their public events.

In 2 Samuel 13-15, David, the "mob boss" of Israel's monarchy, displayed a conspicuous soft spot for Absalom, the son whose very name (אַבְשָׁלוֹם, *ʾabšalom*, "father of peace") functioned as an ironic commentary on his father's conduct. Absalom, having murdered his half-brother Amnon in retribution for the rape of their sister Tamar (2 Samuel 13:28-29), stood guilty of bloodshed. Yet David, rather than submitting to the explicit demands of the divine command, presumed to act as judge and jury. He was not governed by the Command of the Lord but by personal affection and concern for public image. "Compassion," in this case, became a political performance.

This sentimental indulgence produced Absalom's exile (2 Samuel 13:37-38), his calculated return (14:21-33), and ultimately his rebellion (15:1-12), a direct outcome of David's failure to uphold justice. From a human vantage point, David's conduct may appear merciful, loving, or kind. Yet it was not צֶדֶק (*ṣedeq*), righteousness as defined by the Lord's command; it was self-consolation, the נָחַם (*naḥam*) of self-referential human sentimentality.

Such terms must be defined not according to manufactured "meaning," the abstract propaganda we construct in our own minds, but according to their function and itinerary within the scriptural canon itself. Scripture, not human sentiment, must serve as the reference:

> וַתְּכַל דָּוִד הַמֶּלֶךְ לָצֵאת אֶל־אַבְשָׁלוֹם כִּי־נִחַם עַל־אַמְנוֹן כִּי־מֵת
>
> *wayyikleh leb hammelek dawid laṣet ʾel-ʾabšalom ki-niḥam ʿal-ʾamnon ki-met*
>
> *"And the heart of King David longed to go out to Absalom, for he was comforted [*נִחַם *(*niḥam*)] regarding Amnon since he was dead." (2 Samuel 13:39)*

A casual reader might conclude, "Ah, David. What a devoted father, what a model family man." It is almost beyond satire. Yet this is precisely what people do: they transform such episodes into moral exemplars. One can readily imagine, without straining credulity, a church retreat, a funeral sermon, or lecture series extolling David as a paradigm of the "compassionate father," drawing its inspiration from this very verse.

Pharaoh's Schadenfreude and Shared Imperial Destruction (Ezekiel 32:31)

In Luke 8, Legion pleads to be spared from judgment, seeking relief from consequences in place of repentance.

He shows no interest in submitting to Jesus, let alone to the one who commands Jesus. Likewise, in Ezekiel 32, Pharaoh exhibits no inclination to submit to the Lord. Submission is not his function. The text makes clear that God could strike him down a thousand times, and Pharaoh would not suddenly confess, "I must bow to the Lord." Not in Ezekiel 32.

Instead, Pharaoh surveys the ruin of other nations, tyrants whose armies have been annihilated, and beholds them in the depths of Sheol. From this vision he draws a perverse comfort. It is a biblical schadenfreude: a hollow consolation derived from the knowledge that they, too, share his destruction at the bottom of the pit (Ezekiel 32:18-32). This is not repentance; it is self-consolation in the suffering of others, a counterfeit comfort that mirrors the posture of Legion.

אֹתָם יִרְאֶה פַרְעֹה וְנִחַם עַל־כָּל־הֲמוֹנֹה חַלְלֵי־חֶרֶב פַּרְעֹה וְכָל־חֵילוֹ נְאֻם אֲדֹנָי יְהוִה׃

ʾotam yirʾe fardo niḥam ʿal-kol-hamonoh ḥalale-ḥereb fardo wekhol-ḥelo neum ʾadonai yahweh

*"Pharaoh will see them, and he will be comforted [*וְנִחַם *(*weniḥam*)] concerning all his hordes killed by the sword—Pharaoh and his army, declares the Lord God." (Ezekiel 32:31)*

In other words, Pharaoh's posture is this: if I must go down, let them all go down with me. It is solidarity in destruction, not submission to the divine command.

Jerusalem's Lament vs. Imperial Self-Consolation (Lamentations 1:18, 21)

The itinerary of this root brings us to Lamentations, where the destruction of Pharaoh is set in contrast to the destruction of Jerusalem. Jerusalem, having been laid waste, calls for the wrath of God to fall upon her enemies. Unlike Saul and Netanyahu, this functional Jerusalem, in her distress, loves Amalek and the nations, desiring to bestow upon them the gift of Ḥoreb. Yet unlike Pharaoh, who derived twisted and perverse comfort from the judgment of others, her plea in Lamentations issues from unbearable weight. It is the cry of endurance, under pressure.

Here I hear alongside the Apostle Paul on two counts. First, in the juxtaposition of Pharaoh with Jerusalem: Paul presents Jerusalem as the exemplar of sin, so that all nations might be brought under the judgment of the Torah, which brings everything to destruction (Romans 3:9-20). Second, he brings all under this pressure—this ἐπιμονή (*epimone*, "endurance, steadfastness")—so that they might endure beneath the weight until they submit.

Tragically, under the influence, principally, of modern Zionism, this reading is inverted. Instead of encountering their "natural face" in the mirror of Scripture (James 1:23-24), interpreters turn inward to recount their experience of persecution, setting it against the sufferings of others. But that is not the function of Lamentations.

Lamentations is not a meditation on comparative suffering. It is the scriptural school of surrender, of relinquishing every claim to self-justification, of accepting one's wickedness, so as to endure under pressure and confess that there is none but him. In this sense, it is Qur'anic, or rather, the Qur'an accords with Lamentations in its insistence on total submission:

צַדִּיק הוּא יְהוָה כִּי פִיהוּ מָרִיתִי שִׁמְעוּ־נָא כָל־עַמִּים וּרְאוּ מַכְאֹבִי

ṣaddiq hu' yahweh ki fihu mariti šim'u-na kol-'ammim uru' mak'obi

"The Lord is righteous, for I have rebelled against his command. Hear now, all you peoples, and see my pain." (Lamentations 1:18)

This call for vindication is not a boast; it is not self-proclamation. It is the plea placed upon the lips of the harlot city: you accept your wickedness, you acknowledge that you are evil, and **you voice the prophetic utterance, and the Lord acts.** You cry out for the nations to become like you, not in imitating your deeds, but in recognizing that they too are harlots. The call is not to follow your example, O Jerusalem; **you are not the light to the nations.**

It is the Torah that is the light to the nations—the Torah which you rejected. If the nations hear your plea and submit to the Torah, they will not share your fate, O Jerusalem.

שָׁמְעוּ כִּי נֶאֱנָחָה אָנִי אֵין מְנַחֵם לִי כָּל־אֹיְבַי שָׁמְעוּ רָעָתִי שָׂשׂוּ
כִּי אַתָּה עָשִׂיתָ הֵבֵאתָ יוֹם־קָרָאתָ וְיִהְיוּ כָמוֹנִי

šam'u ki ne'enaḥah ani 'en menaḥem li kol-'oybay šam'u ra'ati sasu ki attah 'asita hebe'ta yom-qara'ta weyihyu kamoni

*"People have heard that I groan; there is no one to comfort me [מְנַחֵם (*menaḥem*)]. All my enemies have heard of my*

disaster; they are joyful that you have done it. Oh, that you would bring the day which you have proclaimed so that they will become like me." (Lamentations 1:21)

Quranic Parallel: Iblis's Request for Respite (Quran 7:14-15)

In Qur'an, Sūrat al-Aʿrāf سورة الأعراف "The Heights" or "The Elevated Places" 7:14-15, the same motif appears through a different root structure: أ-م-ر (*alif-mīm-rāʾ*), with Iblīs "begging" God for respite using ن-ظ-ر (*nūn-ẓāʾ-rāʾ*):

قَالَ أنظِرْنِي إِلَىٰ يَوْمِ يُبْعَثُونَ

qāla anẓirnī ilā yawmi yubʿathūn

*"He said, 'Grant me [*أنظِرْنِي *(*anẓirnī*)] respite until the Day they are resurrected.'"*

The functional parallel exposes a cross-textual pattern: imperial and rebellious agents plead not for repentance but for delay. Their petition is a request for temporal extension out of fear, not submission to divine authority. As with Pharaoh in Ezekiel 32 and Legion in Luke 8, the appeal is no act of contrition but a calculated deferral of judgment: a maneuver to preserve autonomy in defiance of the divine command. This stands in stark contrast to the Matthean use of πειρασμός (*peirasmos*) in the Lord's Prayer: "καὶ μὴ εἰσενέγκῃς ἡμᾶς εἰς πειρασμόν" (*kai me eisenegkes hemas eis peirasmon,* "and do not lead us into the day of the test")—Matthew 6:13. The petition implores a postponement that grants opportunity for changed conduct under acquiescence to God as Judge, on the basis of the promise of debt-forgiveness toward others in submission to him, his name be praised.

Scripture's Zero-Sum Proposition

Scripture begins with a zero-sum proposition: will you accept that you are wicked? Can you look into the mirror of Scripture—the mirror James names—and see your natural face, then admit without excuse: I am evil. Full stop. No crisis, no lament, no staged drama. Only the plain acknowledgment, and the courage to sit with it.

The question then becomes: What follows? If you can abide in the awareness of your wickedness, then there is something to discuss. Yet most cannot. All religious, political, and philosophical drama springs from our refusal to accept this judgment, our relentless effort to deny it. And yet the freedom that comes from God begins and ends with this simple acknowledgment of what we are.

The statement sounds severe, even unbearable, yet it is precisely this severity that makes the whole system of wisdom possible. Nothing can be constructed upon it; it is a non-starter by design. It allows no advance, no retreat, no evasion. The prophetic utterance (that we ourselves are the transgression) brings us to a standstill.

Religion, in its institutional form, seeks to domesticate this truth: to redirect it toward the faults of others, thereby rallying followers to one's cause in order to accomplish something deemed "good." But this is not the function of the text. The text declares without qualification that there is a problem with you, and you alone.

Human Evil is Not Banal

We create meaning to evade this encounter. Meaning is our propaganda, our self-justifying construction. But the text does not offer meaning; it confronts us with what is found, what is given by him, what is visited upon us.

II. Triliteral Lexicographical Excavation: ἐπιτάσσω (*epitasso*) / צ־ו־ה (*ṣade-waw-he*) / و-ص-ي (*wāw-ṣād-yā'*)

In Luke 8:31, the verb ἐπιτάσσω (*epitasso*), "to command," "to give an order," "to issue a directive with authority", corresponds in biblical Hebrew to the root צ־ו־ה (*ṣade-waw-he*, "to command") and in Arabic to وَصَّى (*waṣā*, "to enjoin, to instruct"). This root has a discernible itinerary across both the Bible and the Qur'an. Its significance lies in its consistent thematic association with obedience under pressure, whether in the aftermath of destruction or judgment, or in the looming shadow of such judgment.

In either case, obedience becomes the sole path forward, the only viable ground for hope, despite the persistent wickedness of the human being. The command is not contingent upon the moral improvement of the recipient; it demands compliance precisely within the context of human corruption and divine authority.

Command Under Pressure

Patriarchal Testament and Divine Command (Genesis 49:33; Qur'an 2:132)

וַיְכַל יַעֲקֹב לְצַוֹּת אֶת־בָּנָיו וַיֶּאֱסֹף רַגְלָיו אֶל־הַמִּטָּה וַיִּגְוַע וַיֵּאָסֶף אֶל־עַמָּיו

wayyekal ya'aqob leṣawot 'et-banaw wayye'esof raglaw 'el-hammittah wayyigwa' wayye'asef 'el-'ammayw

*"When Jacob finished commanding [*צִוָּה *(*ṣiwāh*)] his sons, he drew his feet into the bed and breathed his last and was gathered to his people." (Genesis 49:33)*

wa-waṣṣā bihā 'Ibrāhīmu banīhi wa-ya'qūbu yā banayya inna allāha iṣṭafā lakumu ad-dīna fa-lā tamūtunna 'illā wa-'antum muslimūn

*"And Abraham enjoined [*وَصَّى *(*waṣṣā*)] it upon his sons, and [so did] Jacob: 'O my sons, indeed God has chosen for you the religion, so do not die except while you are in submission.'" (Qur'an, Sūrat al-Baqarah* سورة البقرة *"The Cow" 2:132)*

PROPHETIC OBEDIENCE UNDER PERSONAL DESTRUCTION (EZEKIEL 24:18)

וָאֲדַבֵּר אֶל־הָעָם בַּבֹּקֶר וַתָּמָת אִשְׁתִּי בָּעָרֶב וָאַעַשׂ בַּבֹּקֶר כַּאֲשֶׁר צֻוֵּיתִי

wa'adabber 'el-ha'am babboqer watamat 'ishti ba'ereb wa'a'as babboqer ka'ašer ṣuweyti

*"So I spoke to the people in the morning, and in the evening, my wife died. And in the morning, I did as I was commanded [*כַּאֲשֶׁר צֻוֵּיתִי *(*ka'ašer ṣuweyti*)]." (Ezekiel 24:18)*

Human Evil is Not Banal

THE STRAIGHT PATH AND DIVINE INJUNCTION (QURAN 6:151, 153)

قُلْ تَعَالَوْا أَتْلُ مَا حَرَّمَ رَبُّكُمْ عَلَيْكُمْ ۖ أَلَّا تُشْرِكُوا بِهِ شَيْئًا وَبِالْوَالِدَيْنِ إِحْسَانًا

qul taʿālaw ʾatlu mā ḥarrama rabbukum ʿalaykum ʾallā tushrikū bihi shayʾan wa-bi-l-wālidayni ʾiḥsānan

*"Say, 'Come, I will recite what your Lord has enjoined [*وَصَّى *(*waṣṣā*)] upon you: that you not associate anything with him, and to parents, good treatment...'"' (Qur'an, Sūrat al-Anʿām* سورة الأنعام *"The Cattle" 6:151)*

وَأَنَّ هَٰذَا صِرَاطِي مُسْتَقِيمًا فَاتَّبِعُوهُ ۖ وَلَا تَتَّبِعُوا السُّبُلَ فَتَفَرَّقَ بِكُمْ عَن سَبِيلِهِ ۚ ذَٰلِكُمْ وَصَّاكُم بِهِ لَعَلَّكُمْ تَتَّقُونَ

wa-anna hādhā ṣirāṭī mustaqīman fa-ittabiʿūhu wa-lā tattabiʿū as-subula fatafarraq bikum ʿan sabīlihi dhālikum waṣṣākum bihi laʿallakum tattaqūn

*"This is my path, straight. So, follow it and do not follow other ways. This he has enjoined [*وَصَّى *(*waṣṣā*)] upon you that you may become righteous." (Qur'an, Sūrat al-Anʿām* سورة الأنعام *"The Cattle" 6:153)*

צַדִּיק הוּא יְהוָה כִּי פִיהוּ מָרִיתִי שִׁמְעוּ־נָא כָל־עַמִּים וּרְאוּ מַכְאֹבִי

ṣaddiq huʾ yahweh ki fihu mariti šimʿu-na kol-ʿammim uruʾ makʾobi

"Righteous is Yahweh, for I have rebelled against his command [lit. 'mouth']. Listen, all peoples, and behold my pain." (Lamentations 1:18)

It is pressure, the imposition of commandment, an authoritative directive that demands obedience unto righteousness. It marks out a singular path, binding the hearer to divine instruction. The Hebrew צ־ו־ה (*ṣade-waw-he*) in Ezekiel 24 and the Qur'anic وَصَّى (*waṣṣā*) in *Sūrat al-An'ām* carry the same functional weight as the Greek ἐπιτάσσω (*epitasso*) in Luke 8:31, to command, order, or issue a directive with binding authority, often to avert judgment or consequence.

Yet the proximity to encounter varies. In Ezekiel 24 and Lamentations, the commandment is given within destruction amid judgment already underway. In Qur'an 6, it is given to prevent destruction. In both situations, hope lies only in complete dependence upon the commandment to direct one's path, whether under the weight of judgment or in the effort to avert it.

LEGION'S MANIPULATION OF DIVINE COMMAND

> *"They were imploring him [παρακαλέω (*parakaleo*)]… (seeking their own consolation, their own comfort, pleading for their own reprieve)…not to command them [ἐπιτάσσω (*epitasso*)]…" (Luke 8:31)*

Here, the plea is not submission but a strategic attempt to manipulate the divine command for personal advantage. The connection to Pharaoh is clear: like Pharaoh in Ezekiel 32, Legion seeks a reprieve on its own terms, not submission to God's terms. This is consistent with the identification of Legion as a cipher for Caesar, the Roman imperial presence.

In the itinerary of the term, the pattern mirrors that of Saul in 1 Samuel 15: the evasion of consequence under the guise of negotiation. The request is not to be spared for the sake of righteousness, but to avoid the authority of the Command itself. This is the perennial posture of those who bend divine authority into human legalism (the Justinian crowd) who treat the Torah not as an unyielding word from the Lord, but as a corpus of statutes to be managed, amended, legislated, or bypassed.

III. ἄβυσσος (*abyssos*) / ת־ה־ם (*taw-he-mem*): The Deep, the Rubble, and Divine Function

> *"...to go away into the abyss [ἄβυσσος (*abyssos*)]." (Luke 8:31)*

For Legion, pleading not to be sent into the ἄβυσσος (*abyssos*) is not a request for mercy in the biblical sense; it is a request to avoid the full imposition of the divine judgment, just as Pharaoh in Ezekiel 32 takes refuge in the company of the other condemned in Sheol. The "abyss" is the terminus of disobedience, the containment of rebellion by divine authority. To remain in Pharaoh's company is to remain in defiance of the Command while trying to mitigate the cost.

Genesis 1:2: תהו ובהו *(***tohu wa-bohu***) vs.* תהום *(***tehom***)—Rubble, Not Philosophical Void*

ἄβυσσος (*abyssos*) in Luke 8:31 corresponds to תְּהוֹם (*tehom*), "the deep", and is lexically bound to תֹהוּ וָבֹהוּ (*tohu wa-bohu*). In the scriptural text, this pairing does not describe a philioshopical pre-creation state but the aftermath of judgment: a land rendered uninhabitable and nonfunctional, awaiting the imposition of the divine command. Genesis 1:2 itself encodes this judgment grammar. *tohu wa-bohu* and *tehom* mark a world already reduced to rubble, into which God speaks function. The prophets apply this language of judgment, making the text circular by design, as Paul wrote, from grace to peace,[40] as in Isaiah 34:11 and Jeremiah 4:23, lands under condemnation are described as returning to *tohu wa-bohu*; and in Ezekiel 26:19-20, תְּהוֹם (*tehom*) submerges Tyre, erasing it from the civlized world of man made order. Thus the "abyss" is not geography but a category of decreation.[41] Legion's plea in Luke 8:31 is therefore a bid to evade this Genesis-encoded judgment. The return to תְּהוֹם (*tehom*) that strips away human ordering and leaves only the rubble awaiting God's command.

In modern terms, it is what we see in the rubble of Gaza: material rendered useless by systematic destruction. After sustained assault, there is desolation, a landscape no longer capable of sustaining life. That is how one must hear Genesis: not as a treatise on the "void," but as an image of ruin. The biblical writers, members of the intelligentsia of their day, understood precisely what imperial systems would do to the poor.

---

[40] Paul opens his epistles with the formula, "Grace to you and peace from God our Father and the Lord Jesus Christ" (χάρις καὶ εἰρήνη, *charis kai eirene*) (Romans 1:7; 1 Corinthians 1:3; 2 Corinthians 1:2; Galatians 1:3; Ephesians 1:2; Philippians 1:2; Colossians 1:2; 1 Thessalonians 1:1; 2 Thessalonians 1:2; Philemon 1:3).

[41] Davidson, Brian W. *The Organic Connection between Rebellion, Decreation, and Divine Judgment* (Eugene, OR: Wipf and Stock, 2021), blog post dated November 27, 2024, discussing how Genesis 6 uses the verb שָׁחַת (*šaḥat*, "to corrupt") four times to connect human rebellion, decreation, and divine judgment, especially in verses 11-14.

Human Evil is Not Banal

They were not speculating about metaphysical emptiness; they were describing the aftermath of siege and conquest. Their vocabulary arose from lived encounter: cities razed, fields stripped bare, and dwellings collapsed into heaps of stone. תֹהוּ וָבֹהוּ (*tohu wa-bohu*) is the prophetic register for such devastation: a deliberate lexical choice that encodes judgment.

Genesis 1:2 and the Creative Word After Destruction

In Genesis 1, תֹהוּ וָבֹהוּ (*tohu wa-bohu*) sets the stage for the Most High God. For the creative word of the Scriptural God. He alone creates. It is his word, and his word alone, that brings order and purpose, that renders rubble functional again through his Command.

> וְהָאָרֶץ הָיְתָה תֹהוּ וָבֹהוּ וְחֹשֶׁךְ עַל־פְּנֵי תְהוֹם וְרוּחַ אֱלֹהִים מְרַחֶפֶת עַל־פְּנֵי הַמָּיִם
>
> *weha'areṣ hayetah tohu wabohu weḥošek 'al-fene tehom weruaḥ 'elohim meraḥefet 'al-fene hammayim*
>
> *"Now the earth was formless and void [*תֹהוּ וָבֹהוּ *(*tohu wa-bohu*)] and darkness over the face of the deep [*תְּהוֹם *(*tehom*)], and the Spirit of God was hovering over the surface of the waters." (Genesis 1:2)*

Here we find the same "deep" (*tehom*) that functions in Luke 8, the ἄβυσσος (*abyssos*) to which Legion begs to be sent. But Legion's plea is not repentance; it is the arrogant resignation of one who accepts destruction only as long as it offers self-consolation. It is the posture of Saul, who spares what he was commanded to destroy, and of Pharaoh, who takes comfort in the shared ruin of others in Ezekiel 32.

Genesis, however, reveals the alternative: the תְּהוֹם (*tehom*) is not only a place of judgment; it is the raw setting for God's creative work after prophetic destruction. Once we accept that in our wickedness we cannot create anything, the hope lies here: "And the Spirit of God was hovering over the surface of the waters."

Ezekiel 26:19: The Deep and the Defunctioning of Tyre

The deep is no casual image in Scripture. In Ezekiel 26, which Luke invokes lexically, תְּהוֹם (*tehōm*) functions to defunction Tyre. It is the instrument of unmaking. Ezekiel submerges the city in language that calls the hearer back to Genesis 1. תֹהוּ (*tohu*) does not appear here, yet the consonantal Hebrew vocabulary makes the Genesis 1 reference unmistakable.

This is the prophetic method: to reduce everything, if only in the imagination, back to rubble, so that the only hope is the divine command. The prophets return us to the state in which God alone is able speak to avert destruction, to make the rubble functional. But we resist the basic premise: that we are wicked, and that this wickedness brought us to destruction.

We cannot hear Jerusalem's lament because we are like Legion. We would rather sit with Pharaoh, savoring the ruin of others, than submit to the divine word. That is what we are.

Nazis.

Human Evil is Not Banal

כִּי כֹה אָמַר אֲדֹנָי יְהוִה בְּתִתִּי אֹתָךְ עִיר נֶחֱרֶבֶת כֶּעָרִים אֲשֶׁר לֹא־
נוֹשָׁבוּ בְּהַעֲלוֹת עָלַיִךְ אֶת־תְּהוֹם וְכִסּוּךְ הַמַּיִם הָרַבִּים

ki koh ʾamar ʾadonai yhwh betiti ʾotak ʿir neḥerebet keʿarim ʾašer lo-nošabu behaʿalot ʿalayik ʾet-tehom wekissuk hammayim harabbim

*"For this is what the Lord Yahweh says: When I make you a desolate city, like the cities which are not inhabited, when I bring up the deep [*תְּהוֹם *(*tehom*)] over you, and the great waters cover you." (Ezekiel 26:19)*

There it is: the תְּהוֹם (*tehōm*) that in Genesis 1 becomes the setting for divine creation, here functions as the agent of destruction. In Luke 8, Legion fears being sent there, not because he seeks repentance, but because he wants to avoid consequence, just as Pharaoh takes refuge in the solidarity of ruin in Ezekiel 32. The deep is the place where God strips away all pretense, bringing the world back to the point where his Command is the only possible organizing principle of life.

Against the Cycle of Death and Resurrection: Exposing Neopagan Distortion

When people say the prophets proclaim a "cycle" of death and resurrection, they utter blasphemy.[42]

---

[42] Cooper, Matthew Franklin. *In the Houses of the Poor.* (St. Paul, MN: OCABS Press, 2025) pp. 228-29. "What follows are all variations on the basic themes already present: that God's provision has been made very good and sufficient for all, and human beings' attempts to limit, control and usurp that provision all end in ignominious failure. Yet human beings in their civilisations persist in making such attempts against God's provision—leading to cycles of confident rise, hubris, decadence and fall."

> *"You see, Father Marc, when you go through the prophets, you realize it's death and resurrection, death and resurrection. It's a cycle."*

This is not biblical teaching; it is neopaganism disguised as exegesis. It is a rejection of the divine command. The refrain "It's a cycle" is simply the voice of an age-old idolatry that sanctifies human self-perpetuation.

Scripture does not glorify natural cycles. It proclaims rubble: the ruin that comes precisely because the divine command was rejected. The destruction of Jerusalem is not merely an event but a proposition: submit to the divine command to break the cycle for the continuation of life. Yet the cycle cannot be broken unless we accept that we are harlots.

The lament, therefore, is not a sentimental meditation on suffering for its own sake. As Paul says, μὴ γένοιτο (*me genoito*), literally "may it never be" or "absolutely not!"[43] It is an appeal to divine vengeance, not as vindictiveness, but as the exposure of harlotry and the undoing of rebellion. The hope is eschatological: on that day, all nations will be under God's command. This is the proposition of Scripture and the true content of the lament.

Staring Into the Abyss of Our Natural Face

Luke 8:31 is a tricky verse. In a cheap sermon, it is easily flattened into talk about baptism or Pharaoh, safe and predictable tropes. But do we truly take the time to

---

[43] (Romans 3:4, 3:6, 3:31; 6:2, 6:15; 7:7, 7:13; 9:14; 11:1, 11:11; 1 Corinthians 6:15; Galatians 2:17; 3:21; 6:14)

stare into the ugly abyss of our natural face in the mirror?

Conclusion

This trilingual lexicographical analysis demonstrates that Luke 8:31 participates in Scripture's systematic exposure of imperial self-consolation. Legion's plea, "They were imploring him not to command them to go away into the abyss", is not merely a parable of demonic activity but part of the broader, consistent pattern of imperial resistance to divine authority. It links Legion, both terminologically and functionally, to:

- Saul's obsession with reputation management and the divine regret that follows.
- David's sentimental criminality disguised as pastoral care.
- Pharaoh's perverse delight in shared destruction.
- Contemporary liberal politicians' measured rhetoric on Gaza while sustaining imperial violence.

The triple constraint of evil, the natural mirror of Scripture, the artificial mirrors of self-flattery, and the blind neighbor who bears witness to our hypocrisy, exposes the ways we construct meaning to evade the divine judgment that demands submission.

Scripture's zero-sum proposition is unambiguous: accept your wickedness or remain trapped in the self-deception that sustains the very evil you claim to resist. The freedom God gives begins and ends with acknowledging what we are. Only then can his Command speak order into the rubble of human pretension.

The convergence of Hebrew, Arabic, and Greek evidence confirms that Luke 8:31 participates in a unified scriptural conversation in which divine authority consistently confronts human imperial pretension. Through the Judaeo-Arabic triliteral root methodology of al-Andalus, we hear the Greek New Testament functioning not as a Hellenistic text, but as Semitic literature participating in inter-functional scriptural discourse without regard for human institutional boundaries.

Can you sit with your wickedness? Can you look at your natural face in the scriptural mirror and not look away? The prophets bring our man made constuctions down to rubble—unto hope—so that God might speak his Command and render the rubble functional again.

Yet most refuse. All the drama arises from our unwillingness to accept what we are. We fight it with all our strength. We are wicked like Legion, preferring to sit with Pharaoh and take perverse comfort in the destruction of others. That is what we are.

The text waits. The mirror is not your friend—but it may be his victory. To gaze steadily into the mirror of Scripture is to reach a decisive point: either turn away in rejection, or finally recognize the face that God, in his mercy, has come to redeem.

Jesus leads a quiet, pastoral intifada
of nomadic shepherds against entrenched urban
elites, with Galilee, the rolling caravan
of the nations, as its cradle.

سُبْحَانَ مَنْ جعَلَ فِي الْحَمْدِ نُورًا

(subḥāna man ja'ala fī al-ḥamdi nūran)
"Glory to the one who placed light within praise"

The Voice of the Shepherd

This is the Voice of the Scriptural God:
The Voice of the Shepherd.
It will not be silenced.
It cannot be bought.
It does not serve a throne.
It does not belong to anyone.
It roams freely upon the earth,
calling its flock from the outlands, out of the city to the wilderness.

The Biblical Jesus is near, Ḥabibi,
And it's time for the Lord to act.

It's time for Ibrahim's Discords.

The Forever War Against Pastoral Peoples

Both the Bible and the Qur'an emerged from nomadic pastoral societies. Yet these same texts were later weaponized by sedentary civilizations against the very peoples once nurtured by them. We are witnessing this tragic pattern unfold again in real time, perhaps in its most brutal form yet, with escalating consequences that now reach into the heart of the West, the heir of Greco-Roman and Crusader hubris.

The Voice of the Shepherd

Even in pre-biblical East Asian traditions such as the Confucian Book of Odes, herdsmen arrive with their flocks to establish an unnamed prince,[44] a figure who emerges not from the city but from the periphery to usher in an era of divine justice. This archetype, consolidated in the Bible and the Qur'an, becomes active in the world whenever and wherever the voice from the pasture rises against the corruption of the palace.

Methodological Framework: Grammatical Excavation Against Narrative Illusion

The Lie of "Narrative" Interpretation

If you are still waiting to hear a narrative, you work with and for the people who are persecuting the poor. There is no narrative. This idolotrous obsession with "narrative" represents the fundamental error of Greco-Roman biblical interpretation, the attempt to reduce divine terminology, which demands lexicographical submission, to human meaning.

Biblical study is work. It is the archaeology of terms, of terminology in the original languages. Everything else is merely people talking about themselves, which concerns the defense and protection of their civilizations, their empires, their identities. In this dynamic, accusations of "identity politics" are frequently directed toward immigrants or minority communities. Yet the implicit assumption of such accusations is that there is only one

---

[44] Cooper, Matthew Franklin. "The lexicology of *lai* 來 and *mai* 麥." *Skeireins*, Substack, July 4, 2025, skeireins. substack. com/ p/ the-lexicology-of-lai-and-mai.

acceptable identity: that of the dominant civilization. The critique is therefore asymmetrical: the identity of the majority is treated as natural, normative, and unassailable, while other identities are cast as divisive, selfish, or political.

But we pertain to the prince, the Confucian prince, the Bedouin shepherd, the biblical Jesus who was cancelled in order to pertain to the unseen Shepherd in the Big Tent in the wilderness.

Each Word is a Universe

Each word in the text is a universe. Forget the Greco-Roman conceit that "each person is a universe." Each artifact in the text, both in its function and its inter-function, connects to a vast itinerary within the three scrolls of Abraham. This is the inexhaustible well, the well of the Samaritan woman referenced later in the Gospel of John (4:1-42; 7:37-39), from which the waters of hearing never cease to flow.

There is not a single word, artifact, or function in Luke 8:32-34 that does not warrant an entire episode, a paper, a project a book! Each term, each function, is an effort, a study, an itinerary, a trail, a breadcrumb. By now, if your "Bible study" consists of simply reading and talking, you are wasting your time. Such exercises are nothing more than people talking about themselves, defending and protecting their own civilizations, empires, and identities.

Archaeological Excavation: ἀγέλη (*agelē*) / ע-ד-ר (*ʿayin-dalet-reš*) / غ-د-ر (*ghayn-dāl-rāʾ*)

*"Now there was a herd [ἀγέλη (*agele*)] of many swine feeding there on the mountain, and the demons implored him to permit them to enter the swine, and he gave them permission." (Luke 8:32)*

The Systematic Mockery of Greco-Roman Moralism

In the Gospel of Matthew, we are told that God will separate the sheep from the goats (25:32). Mishearing this, the rule-followers among us turn their gaze outward, presuming to instruct others on which rules to follow. In so doing, they become goat-finders and goat-fixers: predators, lions and bears, who come not to protect the flock but to steal from it.

This separation imagery excites many. They are certain they know exactly what Matthew means: We must separate the sheep from the goats! Scripture is teaching us how to be sheep, they say, how to follow the law correctly! Such reasoning mirrors the moralism of Roman philosophers, who imagine there is a "right way" to live that consists largely in identifying and correcting the failings of others.

Yet the text does not authorize us to make such distinctions. None of us can separate sheep from goats, we cannot even tell them apart. As Matthew reminds us, the rain falls on both the just and the unjust (5:45). A sheep is a sheep, and a goat is a goat, and at the moment, it is not certain that God has any quarrel with goats whatsoever. You of course, might, which is precisely why you are so eager to correct them.

The same presumption drives the pattern in Luke 8: those who "find" the healed man at Gerasa respond with fear rather than joy. They are not neutral observers, they are finders in the worst sense, rushing to pass judgment where only God has the authority to judge. In Scripture, to "find" often marks the moment when divine action is about to fall—grace if received, judgment if refused. But human finders turn this divine function into an imperial one, policing the flock, sorting sheep from goats, and consolidating their own authority.

In both Matthew and Luke, the warning is clear: you are not the Shepherd. The sorting belongs to God alone. The human task is not to control or classify but to hear, to submit, and to stand in the breach. Anything else is merely another form of empire, whether clothed in moral language, draped in religious zeal, or, worst of all, robed in the garments of civic virtue by the ungodly "community builders."

Luke's Application of ע־ד־ר *(*'ayin-dalet-reš*) from the Song of Songs*

In Luke's application of ע־ד־ר (*'ayin-dalet-reš*) from the Song of Songs, the dichotomy is inverted. When the mashal unfolds in the Decapolis, the Song's poetic use of ἀγέλη (*agele*), interchanging goats and sheep, becomes a satire on human rule-followers. The constant switching between goats and sheep in the Song of Songs reflects a deliberate poetic symmetry: goats evoke movement and allure (expressed in the hair), while sheep evoke purity and precision (the teeth). In love poetry, beautiful hair and beautiful teeth form a harmonious pair. But note carefully, one is associated with the goat, the other with the sheep.

The point is as sharp in Luke as in Matthew: you are not the Shepherd. The sorting belongs to God alone. The Davidic pasture, the wisdom of Proverbs, the romance of the Song, and the confrontations in the Gospels all expose the vanity of those who imagine themselves qualified to judge, reminding us that God alone sees the truth.

Biblical Itinerary of the Herd Function

- **David as Shepherd:** "David said to Saul, 'Your servant was tending his father's flock [הָעֵדֶר (*ha-'eder*)], and when a lion or a bear came and took a sheep from the flock…'" (1 Samuel 17:34)
- **Pastoral Vigilance:** "Know well the condition of your flocks [עֲדָרִים (*'adarim*)] and pay attention to your herds." (Proverbs 27:23)
- **The Beloved's Question:** "Tell me, you whom my soul loves, where do you pasture your flock [עֵדֶר (*'eder*)], where do you have it lie down at noon?" (Song of Songs 1:7)
- **The Goats and Sheep Dialectic:** "Your hair is like a flock [כְּעֵדֶר (*ke'eder*)] of goats, coming down from Mount Gilead" (4:1); "Your teeth are like a flock [כְּעֵדֶר (*ke'eder*)] of newly shorn sheep, which have come up from their watering place" (4:2)

The deliberate vacillation between sheep and goats demonstrates Scripture's mockery of human attempts to establish rigid legal categories.

The Song of Songs and the Impossibility of Systematization

Drawn from pastoral life, the imagery of sheep and goats is repurposed in Luke to mock self-righteous Hellenistic constructs of law. The Greco-Roman instinct is always to hold the weak to account, to press the poor for payment. Paul delights in overturning this instinct, exposing the greed and legalism of his Roman hearers: "Pay to all what is owed to them…" (Romans 13:7). The irony is cutting. What they owe is not extraction from the poor, but submission to the debt of God's command.

But the Song of Songs refuses such control. The beloved is not constrained by boundary, dark and light, wild and ordered, descending and ascending, all coexist in the text. It is a complete pastoral image that cannot be systematized or contained. The beloved is not judged; she is adored. She is delighted in, not corrected. And so, the question presses itself: Is that how you look at the goat, O goat-fixers? Do you see the goat with delight, or merely as something to be fixed?

The Qur'anic Correspondence: Rules of Engagement in Nomadic Society

Even in the open pasture, there are rules of engagement in nomadic life. Qur'an, Sūrat al-Anfāl سورة الأنفال "The Spoils of War" outlines the terms of conflict and the proper conduct of the faithful toward their enemies. It contains the Qur'an's only occurrence of the Lukan-corresponding root غ-د-ر *(ghayn-dāl-rā')*, denoting treachery or betrayal:

The Voice of the Shepherd

*"And if you fear betrayal [*غدرًا (ghadran)*] from a people who stand out [as a group], then cast it back to them on equal terms. Truly, God does not love those who betray."* *(Qur'an 8:58)*

Here the term قَوْم (*qawm*, "those who stand or rise together as a group") derives from the root ق-و-م (*qāf-wāw-mīm*), linked in Hebrew to the "Day of the Lord" and the act of being raised. As we know, Jesus does not rise by his own power, he is raised and seated at the right hand of power.

This imagery resonates with the Decapolis scene in Luke, where the herd of swine, ἀγέλη (*agelē*), stands before Jesus and is driven into the sea. The herd belongs to Caesar; it is Legion's property, an image of law and empire. Its destruction signals the end of the imperial order that persecutes the goats. In this shared pastoral vocabulary, the Qur'an and the Bible converge: it is not the herd that matters, but obedience to the Shepherd.

This obedience is trust in him, the Alpha and Omega, the first step and the final breath, the voice that calls through the storm, the staff that scatters the wolves, the hand that gathers the lost. Outside his call there is only the night, but in his Command the flock lives, moves, and has its function. Submission to him is the center, the circumference, and the whole pasture in between.

Finders, Beware

From David's pasture to the Song's romance, from Matthew's parable to Luke's Decapolis, and in the Qur'anic pasture-law of Sūrat al-Anfāl, the warning is unbroken: you are not the Shepherd. The sorting belongs to God alone. In Scripture, to "find" is never licensed to seize divine authority. It is a summons to submit, grace if received, judgment if refused.

The people of Gerasa, who found the healed man and chose fear over joy, mirror this perennial human failing. Confronted with the disruptive mercy of God's kingdom, they clung to the false peace of empire, unwilling to bear the grace that unmasks their loyalty to injustice. So it is now: political and religious leaders invoke sacred language to buttress the very systems Scripture opposes, silencing the voice that calls them to the pasture of the Shepherd.

Archaeological Excavation: Ὄρος (*oros*) / ה־ר־ר (*he-reš-reš*)

The Complete Geography of Divine Rebellion in Ezekiel

The second critical function in Luke 8:32 is ὄρος (*oros*, "mountain"), corresponding to Hebrew הַר (*har*), which carries a complex textual itinerary throughout Scripture. This is not merely a matter of topography but a system of lexical geography mapping divine judgment against imperial pretension.

The Geography of Rebellion

In Ezekiel, the mountains stand for Israel's high places: altars, shrines, and worship sites condemned for idolatry. God commands Ezekiel to prophesy against them:

The Voice of the Shepherd

> *"Son of man, set your face toward the mountains of Israel [הָרֵי יִשְׂרָאֵל (*hare yisra'el*)] and prophesy against them." (Ezekiel 6:2)*

We have been trained by the Greco-Roman and Crusader-pilgrim tradition to assume that altars and shrines are noble things. Yet in Scripture, they are targets for judgment. The book is good; we are not. When I serve the liturgy at the high place, I know I stand under Ezekiel's condemnation. Most never realize this because they have not heard Ezekiel's voice. But when you serve, Ezekiel is prophesying against you, too, Ḥabibi.

The Geography of Dethroning

When Tyre's ruler claims godlike status, God removes him from his place of power:

> *"I have destroyed you, O covering cherub, from the midst of the stones of fire, and I have cast you as profane from the mountain of God [הַר־אֱלֹהִים (*har elohim*)]." (Ezekiel 28:16)*

The biblical God will not be trifled with. Those who paint him as a "monster" in Western liberal moral discourse do so precisely because his words threaten their self-justifying systems. Yalla, bye.

The Geography of Scattering

The people are dispersed across the mountains, echoing Luke's swine scattered into the abyss:

> *"My flock wandered through all the mountains [עַל־כָּל־הֶהָרִים ('al kol heharim)] and on every high hill." (Ezekiel 34:6)*

This repetition is not for emphasis alone. It is because the message resists acceptance. As James teaches, the human heart instinctively works to forget what it hears, because the words of the text are unbearable.

The Geography of Wrath

The mountain here stands for Edom, against which God stretches out his hand:

> *"Behold, I am against you, Mount Seir [הַר־שֵׂעִיר (har-Se'ir)], and I will stretch out my hand against you." (Ezekiel 35:3)*

In Orthodox funerals, we pray for God to remember, but few realize that this is a prayer for his vengeance, the vindication of Christ and of every abandoned child, from ancient unnamed orphans to Hind Rajab beneath the rubble. Amen.

The Geography of Instruction

After judgment, the mountains receive instruction:

> *"Therefore, you mountains of Israel [הָרֵי יִשְׂרָאֵל (hare yisra'el)], hear the word of the Lord God." (Ezekiel 36:4)*

Western interpreters call this "hope." Scripture calls it instruction, an order that, if resisted, brings destruction.

The Geography of Destruction

On the Day of the Lord, mountains collapse in his wrath:

> *"The mountains shall be thrown down [*וְנָפְלוּ הֶהָרִים *(*wenaflu heharim*)], the steep pathways will collapse, and every wall will fall to the ground." (Ezekiel 38:20)*

Nature is not an independent cycle of death and rebirth; it is subject to the God who controls its collapse.

The Anti-Geography of the Anti-Zion

Ezekiel's eschatological temple is not a restoration of David's Zion but an anti-Zion, perched עַל־רֹאשׁ הָהָר (*ʿal roš hahar*), "on the top of the mountain", beyond the reach of the city and its elites:

- **No King**, not the Zion of the Davidic monarchy.
- **No Priest**, not the Herodian Second Temple.
- **No City**, not the populated, "civilized" Jerusalemite colony.

> *"This is the law of the house: its entire area on the top of the mountain [*עַל־רֹאשׁ הָהָר *(*ʿal roš hahar*)] shall be most holy. Behold, this is the law of the house." (Ezekiel 43:12)*

Why mountains? Because human beings are neopagans who crave something to see. The בָּמוֹת (*bamot*, "high places"), were not about elevation alone but physical reference points for the eye. Ask someone if they believe in God and they will point you to the mountains. Scripture points you instead to the One who made them.

The Third Critical Function: βόσκω (*bosko*, "to feed/pasture") / רָעָה (*ra'ah*) / رعى (*ra'ā*)

This function addresses nomadic pastoral life directly. Shepherding as labor, family duty, and livelihood in the nomadic pastoral landscape. In Luke 8:32, this function is not an abstraction; it is the lived reality of tending, feeding, and guarding the flock.

We are dealing with Jesus as the *locum tenens*: the functional shepherd representing the heavenly Shepherd who is our true pastor and King, his Father. The whole system of Scripture revolves around two camps: the urban elite, who are God's enemies, and the nomadic pastoralists, who always sin against God but are nevertheless the ones God chooses. They remain wicked, but they are the ones with whom God works.

Nomadic Pastoral Life

Labor and Time in Pastoral Life

> *"Behold, it is still high day; it is not time for the livestock to be gathered. Water the sheep, and pasture them [*רעו *(*re'u*)]." (Genesis 29:7)*

This is about pastoral work at a particular time. In the wilderness, time is of the essence because life is constantly at risk. Followers of God's instruction are likened to livestock. They are gathered, scattered, fed, watered, and pastured.

The Voice of the Shepherd

DUTY TOWARD THE FATHER'S FLOCK

> *"While he was still speaking with them, Rachel came with her father's sheep, for she was a shepherdess [רֹעָה (*ro'ah*)]." (Genesis 29:9)*

> *"Then his brothers went to pasture [לִרְעוֹת (*lir'ot*)] their father's flock in Shechem." (Genesis 37:12)*

> *"I am looking for my brothers; please tell me where they are pasturing [רֹעִים (*ro'im*)] the flock." (Genesis 37:16)*

The continual reference to "the father's possession" must be sounded again and again until it shatters the capitalist, egalitarian, Western consumerist mind. You are not the measure. Neither your voice nor mine is the point. It is the Voice of the Shepherd: "My sheep hear my voice, and I know them, and they follow me" (John 10:27). This must be pressed, repeated, driven home until it is grasped, and then rejected, with the full knowledge that the addressee has heard and rebelled.

You doubt your betrayal, yet you do not consider where you sit even now. Upon whose earth was your dwelling raised? The betrayal of the Native peoples is not mere injustice among men; it is an affront against the Lord of the worlds, against the One who gave the scroll to *ahl al-kitāb* (the People of the Book). Doubly so, for it was done in the name of his scroll, which is a scroll of pasture and wandering, a guidance for those who submit. Did not 'Īsā ibn Maryam (Jesus son of Mary) come as a shepherd, a dweller of the wilderness, a man without walls? Yet you adorn him in the garments of empire, making him as a Roman senator. This is blindness to his mission, a denial of who he is, a rejection of the God who sends his messengers as nomads and strangers, never as lords of stone palaces.

> *"You fool! This very night your soul is required of you; and now who will own what you have prepared?'"* *(Luke 12:20)*

Pastoral Imagery in Dreams and Messages

> *"And behold, from the Nile came up seven cows, fine-looking and fat; and they grazed [*רֹעֹת *(*ro'ot*)] in the marsh grass."* *(Genesis 41:2)*

> *"A messenger came to Job and said, 'The oxen were plowing and the donkeys grazing [*רוֹעוֹת *(*ro'ot*)] beside them.'"* *(Job 1:14)*

Harmony Without Laws or Civilization

> *"The cow and the bear will graze [*תִּרְעֶינָה *(*tir'enah*)], their young will lie down together, and the lion will eat straw like the ox."* *(Isaiah 11:7)*

> *"The wolf and the lamb will graze [*יִרְעוּ *(*yir'u*)] together, and the lion will eat straw like the ox; and dust will be the serpent's food."* *(Isaiah 65:25)*

This is the order of creation at peace, free from human grasp. It is not born of treaties or moral projects; it arises only when human interference is withdrawn. When man ceases his futile effort to "fix the goats," harmony appears of itself, or perhaps the bear devours the cow. Either way, it is no concern of yours. You are not God.

The Voice of the Shepherd

The Sufficiency of God

LAMBS GRAZING IN ABANDONED RUINS

*"Then the lambs will graze [*רָעוּ *(*ra'u*)] in their pasture, and strangers will eat in the ruins of the wealthy." (Isaiah 5:17)*

This is God's good news in Scripture, his propriety, his claim, though it will never sound like good news to human ears. To us, even to the poor, it is loss, ruin, humiliation. As Jeremiah testifies, "From the least of them to the greatest of them, everyone is greedy for unjust gain" (Jeremiah 6:13). What we call disaster, God calls justice. What we mourn as collapse, he proclaims as victory for the sake of his name. As Ezekiel declares again and again: "Then they shall know that I am the Lord" (Ezekiel 6:7).

THE POOR GRAZE IN SECURITY AMID JUDGMENT

*"Those who are most helpless of the poor will graze [*יִרְעוּ *(*yir'u*)], and the needy will lie down in security." (Isaiah 14:30)*

GOD BRINGS WIDE PASTURE

*"Then he will give you rain for your seed...and on that day your livestock will graze [*יִרְעֶה *(*yir'eh*)] in a wide pasture." (Isaiah 30:23)*

THE SCATTERED FEED ALONG THE HIGHWAYS

*"They will feed [*יִרְעוּ *(*yir'u*)] along the roads, and their pasture will be on all bare heights." (Isaiah 49:9)*

GOD GATHERS AND SCATTERS

> *"He who scattered Israel will gather him, and he will keep him as a shepherd [*יִרְעֶה *(*yir'eh*)] does his flock." (Jeremiah 31:10)*

God is the Shepherd, as Ezekiel proclaimed, "I myself will be the shepherd of my sheep" (Ezekiel 34:15). The clash in the Decapolis between Jesus and Legion is no mere exorcism. It is the confrontation of a Palestinian shepherd against the might of a Roman oppressor. The pasture of the flock stands against the legions of empire, and the decree is clear: there is no shepherd but God, and no voice but his. As the Noble Qur'an testifies, "God is the best of protectors, and he is the most merciful of the merciful" (Qur'an, Sūrat Yūsuf سورة يوسف "Joseph" 12:64).

Judgment of the Urban Elite (False Shepherds)

FEEDING THEMSELVES

> *"Woe, shepherds of Israel who have been feeding [*הָרֹעִים *(*haro'im*)] themselves! Should the shepherds not feed [*יִרְעוּ *(*yir'u*)] the flock?" (Ezekiel 34:2)*

> *"You slaughter the fat sheep without feeding [*תִרְעוּ *(*tir'u*)] the flock." (Ezekiel 34:3)*

> *"The shepherds fed [*רָעוּ *(*ra'u*)] themselves and did not feed [*רָעוּ *(*ra'u*)] my flock." (Ezekiel 34:8)*

The Voice of the Shepherd

DETHRONED BY DVINE DECREE

> *"I will remove them from feeding [*מְרְעֹת *(*mereʿot*)] sheep. So, the shepherds will not feed [*יִרְעוּ *(*yirʿu*)] themselves anymore." (Ezekiel 34:10)*

The Voice of the Shepherd

> *"I will bring them…and I will feed them [*אֶרְעֶם *(*ʾaraʿem*)] on the mountains of Israel." (Ezekiel 34:13)*

> *"I will feed them [*אֶרְעֶם *(*ʾaraʿem*)] in a good pasture, and their grazing ground will be on the mountain heights." (Ezekiel 34:14)*

> *"I myself will feed [*אֶרְעֶה *(*ʾerʿeh*)] my flock and I myself will lead them to rest." (Ezekiel 34:15)*

> *"But the fat and the strong I will eliminate. I will feed them [*אֶרְעֶם *(*ʾaraʿem*)] with judgment." (Ezekiel 34:16)*

In Scripture, to be fed is not necessarily a sign of favor. The question is always: What are you being fed? This is the decisive measure in the context of divine judgment. The prophets show both sides: the sheep of God's pasture who feed securely (Ezekiel 34:14-15), and the nations who, like Pharaoh, are thrown down as carrion for the birds of the air and the beasts of the field (Ezekiel 32:4). The Qur'an intensifies the same warning: on the Day of Judgment some will be given blessed food: fruits, pure drink, and peace (Qur'an, Sūrat al-Wāqiʿah سورة الواقعة "The Inevitable" 56:20-21), while others will be fed only زقوم (*zaqqūm*), the bitter tree that "boils in the bellies like molten brass" (Qur'an, Sūrat al-Ṣāffāt سورة

الصافات "Those Who Set the Ranks" 37:62-66; Sūrat al-Dukhān سورة الدخان "The Smoke" 44:43-46).

Feeding, then, is judgment. To eat from the Shepherd's hand is to live; to eat the food of wrath is to perish. This is the divine irony: the same act, being fed, divides between life and destruction. Blessed are those whom God feeds in his pasture; woe to those fed with the food of their own rebellion, "eating and drinking their own damnation." (1 Corinthians 11:29)

The suppression of nomadic peoples is an ancient and ongoing reality. Civilization continues to depend on exploiting these simple people who live as God intended. Even now, Gaza testifies, they are made to suffer to sustain our ungodly lifestyles.

Part III

ارجع تائبًا إلىٰ مأوىٰ الرحمة

irji῾ tā᾿iban ilā ma᾿wā al-raḥma

"Return repentant to the abode of mercy"

The Desert Knows His Name

Unfound beneath the moonlit sky, an exile walks unseen among mingled peoples, where mercy leads the obedient, and the light of decree unveils the reckoning.

Mercy and Rebellion

In Scripture, to "find" is never mere discovery. It constitutes encounter, a pivotal moment in the text where mercy confronts rebellion, where divine grace intersects with divine wrath. In Gerasa, the people find the healed man—clothed, rational, silent—and they tremble. He serves as a mirror, a testimony they cannot endure. Restoration becomes scandal. Mercy becomes threat, as indeed it should.

They dismiss the one who scattered their demons precisely because he disturbed their peace. The Scriptures reveal a fundamental truth that reverberates through both Hebrew and Arabic textual traditions: To find a man is to stand at the threshold of wrath, to be weighed, observed, and measured. Will you be spared?

In Hebrew, the root מ־צ־א (*mem-ṣade-aleph*) encompasses finding, meeting, and exposing. In Arabic, the cognate و-ج-د (*wāw-jīm-dāl*) carries the same semantic field. To find, certainly, but also to be discovered, to be found wandering, to be guided. The disbeliever finds God waiting, and no one can shield him. Every expectation collapses under the weight of divine wisdom.

Everything found proves double-edged: Grace, if received. Judgment, if refused. Therefore, finders beware. The light of instruction burns.

The Self-Mutilation of Western Scholarship

ἐξῆλθον δὲ ἰδεῖν τὸ γεγονὸς καὶ ἦλθον πρὸς τὸν Ἰησοῦν, καὶ εὗρον καθήμενον τὸν ἄνθρωπον ἀφ’ οὗ τὰ δαιμόνια ἐξῆλθεν ἱματισμένον καὶ σωφρονοῦντα παρὰ τοὺς πόδας τοῦ Ἰησοῦ, καὶ ἐφοβήθησαν. ἀπήγγειλαν δὲ αὐτοῖς οἱ ἰδόντες πῶς ἐσώθη ὁ δαιμονισθείς. καὶ ἠρώτησεν αὐτὸν ἅπαν τὸ πλῆθος τῆς περιχώρου τῶν Γερασηνῶν ἀπελθεῖν ἀπ’ αὐτῶν, ὅτι φόβῳ μεγάλῳ συνείχοντο· αὐτὸς δὲ ἐμβὰς εἰς πλοῖον ὑπέστρεψεν.

“The people went out to see what had occurred and came to Jesus and found (εὗρον, heuron*) the man from whom the demons had gone out sitting at the feet of Jesus clothed and in his right mind. And they became frightened. Those who had seen it reported to them how the man who had been demon-possessed had been made well. And all the people of the territory of the Gerasenes and the surrounding region asked him to leave them, because they were overcome with great fear; and he got into a boat and returned.” (Luke 8:35-37)*

A Systematic Campaign of Erasure

Ignorance and illiteracy are distinct from lack of intelligence. We conflate these concepts because Western scholarship abounds with brilliant minds. Brilliant minds who, due to the events of 1492, and in the service of imperialism, have become illiterate and ignorant in matters of linguistics and numerous other fields of study. We have amputated scholarship. We have severed key segments of the Western library through a systematic, programmatic campaign of erasure.

This amputation, and I employ this term deliberately, following Paul’s warning in Galatians about those who would mutilate the body in service of tribe, represents more than mere academic oversight. It constitutes what we might characterize as scholarly castration, the deliberate severing of organs essential to the body's proper function. As Paul warns concerning those who trouble the Galatians:

> *ὄφελον καὶ ἀποκόψονται οἱ ἀναστατοῦντες ὑμᾶς. (Galatians 5:12)*
>
> *ophelon kai apokopsontai hoi anastatountes hymas.*
>
> *"I wish those who trouble you would mutilate themselves."*

The systematic exclusion of Arabic and Islamic scholarship from biblical studies represents precisely such mutilation of the scholarly corpus.

Beyond the lip service of pluralism and inclusion (the very same that facilitates genocide) the system of erasure that we have come to understand in our American context—identified by numerous distinguished American writers and historians with respect to Native Americans and African Americans—manifests in the memory hole of our twenty-four-hour news cycles. Likewise, we rightly critique monoculture and the melting pot ideology. We all perceive it. We all bear the wound. We have unmentionables in our culture. We recognize their existence. We don't let them appear on stage at the DNC.

Yet we fail to grasp the full extent of the damage inflicted. We do not perceive how it cripples us intellectually, how it corrupts our scholarship. We fail to understand how intelligence and cleverness prove not merely inadequate but transform into arrogance on a grand scale that facilitates violence when it performs self-mutilation, which occurs when the Spanish crown attempts to erase the brotherhood, the fellowship, the cooperation that existed for centuries between the sons of Noah.

THE LOST LEGACY OF AL-ANDALUS

The scholars of al-Andalus, in fulfillment of Pauline table fellowship, constitute the fathers of linguistics, philology, contemporary biblical scholarship, and literary criticism. These disciplines exist entirely due to the flourishing interaction between the Bible and the Qur'an that took place before being erased and later purged by empire. There has persisted a systematic campaign by Crusaders, orientalists, and by Greco-Roman theology to ignore not only the Hebrew text, but to forget and erase the importance of the cooperation between Islamic and Jewish scholars that gave rise to what we call biblical studies and linguistics.

These fields of study cannot exist without the interaction of these two languages within the context of the inter-functional study of the Bible and the Qur'an. Hebrew and Arabic share a grammatical core rooted in three-letter consonantal anatomies. As I explained earlier, it was the scholars of al-Andalus who fully documented the Lord's grammar, developing a definitive methodology that shaped both Biblical and Qur'anic linguistic scholarship.

The wound runs deep. The militant centuries-long campaign to pretend the Qur'an does not exist means that even now, to consider what remains evident in the words of God, what the fathers of al-Andalus taught us about God's Semitic grammar found in the womb, that the triliteral creates interconnection between his scrolls, to even consider this remains shunned.

This constitutes not laziness but something beyond racism. It represents evil. It embodies a rejection of the teaching of the Apostle Paul. It constitutes a sin against the Holy Spirit.[45] And it manifests as willful ignorance. All because people cling to their tribal identities, because they love their civilizations and their monocultures more than they love God and, by extension, more than they love their neighbor: the Command upon which the whole law and all the prophets rest.

The Missing Organs of Western Scholarship

The time has come to explain this, drawing upon the work of Blaise Webster and Matthew Franklin Cooper after the publication of *Dark Sayings.* For in the present darkness that surrounds us, the moment is urgent: we must turn back to the words of God, for only his utterance illumines the path.

The amputation represents more than academic oversight. When we interact with these texts, we fail to perceive that organs are missing from the body of the West because, at our core, we refuse to accept that we are not the reference point. We are not the Maker. We are not the Creator. Westerners, even the most devout, do not believe in Almighty God. They believe in themselves. That is why they cannot recognize what is missing from what they did not create. I state this with full conviction.

---

[45] This reference draws from Jesus's warning in Matthew 12:31-32 about unforgivable sin, applied here to willful rejection of evident fact.

Writing Dictionaries, Not Interpretations

The Limits of Interpretive Authority

On countless occasions, whether in the podcast or in sermons, I have mocked the pious habit of psychologizing Luke's account: "and all the people of the territory of the Gerasenes and the surrounding region asked him to leave them" (Luke 8:37). The move to personalize or spiritualize this text with the sentimental refrain, "people don't want to be healed," misses the point entirely. With respect to the text, who cares what people want?

Obviously, in personal conversation with someone, a decent person would focus intensely on another's needs, because that constitutes your responsibility as a person of integrity, but with respect to the mashal, only what God wants matters.

The Work of Dictionary Compilation

When we take up his scroll, our labor is not interpretation but lexicon. We are endlessly writing dictionaries. That is the work. We are not explaining what the Bible "means." We have no such authority. Our task is to trace word usage, to record what we find, to hand it on. Nothing more. And yet in this very discipline, in the meticulous study of usage, both we and those with whom we share our study are enabled to hear, not our explanations, but what God said. And in these three verses printed above in translation, which we know is not the words of God but rather a translation, we must return to the original language. I will continue saying this because I know that as often as I say it, it takes considerable time to hear it because it took considerable time for me to hear it. And people much more intelligent than I remain ignorant because they still do not accept that part of their body has been amputated.

The Root מ־צ־א (*mem-ṣade-aleph*) and Its Arabic Cognate

Linguistic Foundations

The term εὑρίσκω (*heurisko*) corresponds to the. Hebrew triliteral מ־צ־א (*mem-ṣade-aleph*). In Arabic the cognate is constructed of different consonants و-ج-د (*wāw-jīm-dāl*) but it remains cognate.[46] This function pertains to finding or reaching, to meeting by chance, to obtaining, to achieving.

The business of finding proves tricky in Scripture because of its intersection with philosophical notions in Hellenism and in mysticism of "finding" God. The concept is absurd. Finding God? The assertion defies credibility. You find nothing. It constitutes a trap. As Paul states clearly in Galatians, you do not know God. You are known by him:

νῦν δὲ γνόντες θεόν, μᾶλλον δὲ γνωσθέντες ὑπὸ θεοῦ

nyn de gnontez theon, mallon de gnosthentes hypo theou

---

[46] Klein, Ernest D., *A Comprehensive Etymological Dictionary of the Hebrew Language for Readers of English* (Jerusalem: Carta, 1987). While Hebrew מ־צ־א and Arabic و-ج-د are cognates sharing semantic fields, they represent different consonantal constructions within the Semitic language family.

"But now that you have come to know God, or rather to be known by God" (Galatians 4:9)

The Trap of Seeking

Notice what happens every time someone comes to church. They are seeking. And you all applaud it, because you are neopagans. If you are "seeking God," it means you are following the darkness of the light in your own eyes. But according to Jesus, "The eye is the lamp of your body; when your eye is clear, your whole body also is full of light; but when it is bad, your body also is full of darkness" (Luke 11:34).

ὁ λύχνος τοῦ σώματός ἐστιν ὁ ὀφθαλμός

ho lychnos tou somatos estin ho ophthalmos

"The eye is the lamp of the body" (Matthew 6:22)

The declaration "I'm seeking"[47] raises the question: How do you address the problem of the darkness in the lamp of your eye? You replace it with the light that comes not from you. Which means that you're no longer seeking. You are found.

Reference. You must change the reference point. And once you are no longer the reference point, you cease seeking to be important in the equation. And that explains why the western library is missing an entire section. And that explains why no matter how intelligent you are, you remain ignorant. Intelligence alone proves insufficient.

---

[47] See my discussion of the Hebrew דָּרַשׁ (*daraš*) in *Dark Sayings* and of "seek and ye shall find" in *Torah to the Gentiles*.

The people find the healed man מ־צ־א (*mem-ṣade-aleph*) and become afraid because they are confronted. They are encountering, not experiencing. They are not the reference point. They are under divine judgment.[48]

Found the Man: Divine Entrapment and Biblical Patterns

The Sign of Divine Action

The one who is healed stands as both judgment and mercy: restored, then sent forth as witness. In Scripture, whenever a man is found, whether by chance encounter, deliberate search, or divine appointment, it is never casual. Finding always precedes entrapment. It is the moment of redirection, of confrontation, of exposure. This is not conjecture. It is the functionality of word usage in the text.

The encounter with this man follows the biblical pattern: to find a man is itself a sign. It marks the onset of God's action, which in Scripture is never "good news." It is judgment breaking in.

Joseph: Found Wandering, Set on Suffering's Path

Joseph, who was found wandering, was set on a path of suffering. For what purpose? To deliver many from famine. A man found him; indeed, he was wandering in

[48] This methodological commitment to word usage rather than interpretive authority reflects traditional approaches to biblical scholarship emphasizing lexicography over hermeneutics.

the field and the man asked him, "What are you looking for?" Is it merely a question?

וַיִּמְצָאֵהוּ אִישׁ וְהִנֵּה תֹעֶה בַּשָּׂדֶה וַיִּשְׁאָלֵהוּ הָאִישׁ לֵאמֹר מַה־תְּבַקֵּשׁ

wayyimṣaʾehu ʾîš wehinnah toʿeh bassadeh wayyiš ʾalehu haʾîš leʾmor mah-tebaqeš

"A man found him, and behold, he was wandering in the field; and the man asked him, 'What are you looking for?'" (Genesis 37:15)

This seemingly simple inquiry hides a deep and unsettling truth. The finding of Joseph wandering in the field represents a divine appointment disguised as chance encounter. The man who finds him redirects Joseph toward his brothers, setting in motion the entire sequence of events that will lead to slavery, suffering, and ultimately the salvation of many from famine. The "finding" (וַיִּמְצָאֵהוּ, *wayyimṣaʾehu*) becomes the pivot point of biblical plot.

Benjamin: "Found Out" by Divine Design

Benjamin was found out by a cup deftly planted. *Found out.* The finding exposed guilt, yet it pressed toward submission, a word despised by erudite Westerners who dwell in libraries long severed from the divine roots. But in Genesis 44, submission leads to reconciliation:

וַיְחַפֵּשׂ בַּגָּדוֹל הֵחֵל וּבַקָּטֹן כִּלָּה וַיִּמָּצֵא הַגָּבִיעַ בְּאַמְתַּחַת בִּנְיָמִן

wayyeḥaffes baggadul heḥel ubaqqaton killah wayyimmaṣʾe haggabiyaʿ beʾamtaḥat binyamin

"He searched, beginning with the eldest and ending with the youngest, and the cup was found in Benjamin's sack" (Genesis 44:12)

We move from Genesis 37 with Joseph to Genesis 44 with Benjamin. He was exposed and he did not rebel. He submitted. He was a *submitter*. And this constituted good news for God.

The contrast proves instructive: Benjamin's response to being "found out" (וַיִּמָּצֵא, *wayyimmaṣ'e*) differs dramatically from typical human reaction. Rather than protest his innocence or rage against injustice, Benjamin submits. This submission, the verbal root of "muslim", transforms exposure into redemption, guilt into reconciliation.

The Prophet: Found Under the Oak

Now we turn to 1 Kings, the prophet found under the oak faces judgment for disobedience. The finding here constitutes a trap. In this case, it's not a trap for the wicked, but for the prophet who fails to remain obedient to God's direct command:

וַיֵּלֶךְ אַחַר אִישׁ הָאֱלֹהִים וַיִּמְצָאֵהוּ יֹשֵׁב תַּחַת הָאֵלָה

wayyelek aḥar 'iš ha'elohim wayyimṣa'ehu yošeb taḥat ha'elah

*"He went after the man of God and found him [וַיִּמְצָאֵהוּ (*wayyimṣa'ehu*)] sitting under an oak" (1 Kings 13:14)*

You shall not eat bread nor drink water nor return by the way you came. Thus, plainly, he was told not to do it. But the prophet was stubborn.

That characterizes how people behave. Now, you could argue that he was tricked or misled or deceived, but all he had to do was follow simple instruction, and he did not. In verse 19, he went back with him and ate bread in his house and drank water. Quite clear in verse 9: you shall not eat bread or drink water or return by the way you came. And what did he do? He went back with him and ate bread in his house and drank water. One finds comic relief in this.

Jonah: Found a Ship, Caught in Divine Storm

Jonah, who finds a ship, is caught in a storm of God's judgment and becomes a reluctant prophet. But Jonah rose up to flee and found a ship going to Tarshish:

וַיָּקָם יוֹנָה לִבְרֹחַ תַּרְשִׁישָׁה מִלִּפְנֵי יְהוָה וַיֵּרֶד יָפוֹ וַיִּמְצָא אָנִיָּה בָּאָה תַרְשִׁישׁ

wayyaqam yonah libroaḥ taršišah millifnei yahweh wayyered yafo wayyimṣaʾ ʾaniyyah baʾah taršiš

"But Jonah rose up to flee to Tarshish from the presence of the Lord, and went down to Joppa and found a ship going to Tarshish" (Jonah 1:3)

Jonah, the reluctant prophet, remained a submitter in spite of himself. His resistance could not undo his yielding to the Command of the Lord. We know you, Jonah. We know your weakness. And yet we know also that you found favor, as did the Ninevites, who turned at the word of God. Scripture proclaims it, and the Qur'an affirms it: "And indeed, Jonah was among the messengers. When he fled to the laden ship, they cast lots and he was among the losers. Then the fish swallowed him while he was blameworthy…And we sent him to a hundred thousand or more, and they believed, so we gave them enjoyment for a time" (Qur'an, Sūrat al-Ṣāffāt سورة الصافات "Those Who Set the Ranks" 37:139-148).

The irony permeates Jonah's mashal: he finds (וַיִּמְצָא, *wayyimṣa'*) exactly what he seeks, escape, yet discovers that divine appointment cannot be evaded through human schemes. The ship he finds becomes the vessel of his encounter with divine judgment, not his escape from it.

Methodological Precision

I return always to the categories of itinerary and function,[49] for without them the import of a term cannot be grasped. To neglect them is to remain ensnared within the vacuous chamber of the Greco-Roman and Crusader universe, whose interpretive framework collapses under its own absurdities. Jerome, to his credit, refused to be confined by the complacencies of his Greco-Roman colleagues, preoccupied as they were with defending "civilization."[50] Wisely, he went and

[49] The emphasis on "itinerary and function" reflects the methodological approach of tracing word usage patterns across biblical texts rather than imposing external meanings.

[50] See Cooper, Matthew Franklin, "The Only *ṭûr 'ahabôt* Worth Discussing…and What We Orthodox Somehow Manage to Get Right about the στιχηρά," February 2 2025, citing Augustine of Hippo, Letter 71 to Jerome, in Letters, trans. Henry Wace and

studied Hebrew with the rabbis in Palestine. There were a few bright spots in a dimly lit chamber.

Found Favor: Standing in the Breach

From Legion to Grace

We move from "found the man" as a use case of this function to finding favor in Luke 8, after Jesus casts out Legion. The significance is sharpened here: Legion is not simply a demonic name but a cipher for the Roman military order, which itself embodies the tyranny of Greco-Roman law and philosophy. In this framework, the casting out of Legion marks not only a healing but a decisive rejection of the juridical and philosophical structures that enslave nomadic peoples under Greco-Roman civilization. Thus, the act of "finding favor" emerges in direct counterpoint to "finding" under the dominion of law and philosophy, signaling divine mercy in place of imperial control.

Jesus casts out Legion and then the people come and find the man sitting at Jesus's feet clothed and in his right mind. Do they rejoice? Certainly not. They never rejoice because they are cowards. They do not celebrate the mercy extended. They are seized with fear. They do not celebrate the restoration. They ask Jesus to leave. It constitutes rebellion.

Philip Schaff, vol. 1 of *Nicene and Post-Nicene Fathers* (Oxford: Parker; New York: Christian Literature Co., 1890-1900), in which Augustine discourages Jerome from translating directly from Hebrew, urging reliance on the Septuagint to avoid discord between Latin and Greek churches.

The Pattern of Rejection

It typifies the עֵדָה *(ʿedah)* that Jesus scatters throughout the gospel of Luke.[51] Grace is repeatedly offered and then rejected. Again, it represents a recurring pattern in the Bible centered around the root מ־צ־א (*mem-ṣade-aleph*) signifying finding, meeting, encountering. You find favor מָצָא חֵן (*maṣaʾ ḥen*) in God's sight. When a character in the story finds favor, it leads to intercession on behalf of the wicked. This represents another interesting function of this root.

Abraham: Pleading for Sodom

Some examples of this prove powerful. Abraham, for example, pleads for Sodom upon finding favor in God's sight. This appears in Genesis 18:

> וַיֹּאמַר אֲדֹנָי אִם־נָא מָצָאתִי חֵן בְּעֵינֶיךָ אַל־נָא תַעֲבֹר מֵעַל עַבְדֶּךָ
>
> *wayyomer ʾadonay ʾim-naʾ maṣaʾti ḥen beʿeyneka ʾal-naʾ taʿabor meʿal ʿabdeka*
>
> *"My lord, if I have found favor in your sight, do not pass by your slave" (Genesis 18:3)*

Abraham's discovery of divine favor immediately transforms into intercession for the wicked. The finding of favor (מָצָאתִי חֵן, *maṣaʾti ḥen*) does not terminate in self-satisfaction but opens into advocacy for others. This

[51] The Hebrew עדה *(ʿedah)* refers to assembly or congregation, used here to describe communities that Jesus scatters rather than gathers, or from which he is turned away.

pattern will repeat throughout Scripture with remarkable consistency.

Lot: Surrounded by Destruction

You have another example with Lot. He is surrounded by destruction and acknowledges or appeals to divine mercy. This appears in Genesis 19:

הִנֵּה־נָא מָצָא עַבְדְּךָ חֵן בְּעֵינֶיךָ וַתַּגְדֵּל חַסְדְּךָ אֲשֶׁר עָשִׂיתָ עִמָּדִי

hinneh-naʾ maṣaʾ ʿabdeka ḥen beʿeyneka wattagdel ḥasdeka ʾašer ʿasita ʿimmadi

"Behold, your slave has found favor in your sight, and you have magnified your kindness" (Genesis 19:19)

Thus, the term appears in connection with Abraham and Lot, and again with Moses, marking continuity in its scriptural itinerary.

Moses: Interceding for the Rebellious Collective

You have a third character in the story repeatedly interceding for Israel's rebellious collective. I deliberately avoid the word "community," as it stands in opposition to Scripture. It is a term of modern usage that undermines the biblical distinction between God's flock and man's swarm. The collective pertains to the reference. You are collected by him. Moses intercedes for the rebellious collective after finding favor in God's sight. This appears in Numbers 11:11:

וַיֹּאמֶר מֹשֶׁה אֶל־יְהוָה לָמָה הֲרֵעֹתָ לְעַבְדֶּךָ וְלָמָּה לֹא־מָצָאתִי חֵן בְּעֵינֶיךָ לָשׂוּם אֶת־מַשָּׂא כָּל־הָעָם הַזֶּה עָלָי

wayyomer moše ʾel-yahweh lamah hareʿota leʿabdeka welamah loʾ maṣaʾti ḥen beʿeyneka lasum ʾet-massa kol-haʿam hazzeh ʿalay

"Moses said to the Lord, 'Why have you dealt ill with your servant? And why have I not found favor in your sight, that you lay the burden of all this people on me?'" (Numbers 11:11)

In the golden calf incident, no favor is found in God's sight, only consequence. Yet Moses stands in the breach, so to speak, to appeal. He intercedes:

וְעַתָּה אִם־מָצָאתִי חֵן בְּעֵינֶיךָ הוֹדִעֵנִי נָא אֶת־דְּרָכֶךָ

weʿattah ʾim-maṣaʾti ḥen beʿeyneka hodiʿeni naʾ ʾet-derakeka

"Now therefore, if I have found favor in your sight, please show me now your ways" (Exodus 33:13)

Esther: The Submitter

Esther, having found favor, risks her life. She is a submitter, made all the more notable by the tragic comedy of her being weaponized by Israeli nationalists, as they do with so many biblical figures. Yet Esther was functionally a muslim not in any institutional or religious sense, but in the verbal sense: she submitted. I realize this strikes many as scandalous, but that is only because they remain ignorant of the text, as I have shown. The term here carries no religious identity; the claim is purely linguistic.

אִם־עַל־הַמֶּלֶךְ טוֹב וְאִם־מָצָאתִי חֵן לְפָנָיו וְכָשֵׁר הַדָּבָר לִפְנֵי הַמֶּלֶךְ

ʾim-ʿal-hammelek ṭob weʾim-maṣaʾti ḥen lefanaw wekašer haddabar lipnei hammelek

"If it pleases the king, and if I have found favor in his sight, and if the thing seems right before the king" (Esther 8:5)

The Cowardice of the Gerasenes

In the mashal of the Gerasenes, the people ask Jesus to leave. They are interested in the survival of their church, so to speak, of their local parish, of their town, of their city. Again, they are cowards. That is what people desire. They want their עֵדָה *(ʿedah)*, their swarm, their herd, their assembly, to survive. They do not appreciate what happened to the swine. (Luke 8:33)

"But Father Marc, if you keep preaching the gospel, the parish will never grow. The problem is you, Father Marc."

I know I am the problem.
I am well aware.
I am not unintelligent.
Not at all, Ḥabibti.
But there is a text here.
So, what do you love more? Yourself, which is what you call "community", or God?
This is an important question.
It is *the* question.

It is also the value of Esther. She demonstrated the one whom she loved. The one who found favor stood in the breach.

But the Gerasenes were cowards.

They rejected the one who stood up and interceded against the Roman legion.

They were *cowards*.

Echoing Israel's Wilderness Rebellion

Their response echoed Israel's rebellion in the wilderness when the people grumbled against Moses:

מִי־יִתֵּן מוּתֵנוּ בְיַד־יְהוָה בְּאֶרֶץ מִצְרַיִם בְּשִׁבְתֵּנוּ עַל־סִיר הַבָּשָׂר בְּאָכְלֵנוּ לֶחֶם לָשֹׂבַע כִּי־הוֹצֵאתֶם אֹתָנוּ אֶל־הַמִּדְבָּר הַזֶּה לְהָמִית אֶת־כָּל־הַקָּהָל הַזֶּה בָּרָעָב

mi-yitten mutenu beyad-yahweh beʾereṣ miṣrayim bešibtenu ʿal-sir habasar beʾokhlenu leḥem lasovaʿ ki-hotseʾtem otanu ʾel-hammidbar hazzeh lehamit ʾet-kol-haqahal hazzeh baraʿab

"Would that we had died by the hand of the Lord in the land of Egypt, when we sat by the meat pots and ate bread to the full, for you have brought us out into this wilderness to kill this whole assembly with hunger" (Exodus 16:3)

The people had just been delivered. But they wanted the safety and security of slavery rather than trust in the provision of God.

As the Apostle Paul taught us, there is no God but one. His name alone be praised. He is our Provider:

εἴδομεν ὅτι οὐδὲν εἴδωλον ἐν κόσμῳ, καὶ ὅτι οὐδεὶς θεὸς εἰ μὴ εἷς eidomen hoti ouden eidolon en kosmo, kai hoti oudeis theos ei me heis

"We know that 'an idol has no real existence,' and that 'there is no God but one'" (1 Corinthians 8:4)

They did not trust in the provision of this God. Likewise in Luke, when confronted with divine mercy in the healed man—Jesus who overturned Rome's chariots just as Moses drowned Pharaoh's chariots—they recoiled in fear and drove him away. Their cry is the same as their fathers': "We were better off in Egypt; leave us alone" (cf. Exodus 14:12; Numbers 14:4). Such is the cowardice of those who love bondage. They turn away from deliverance, as those before them who rejected the prophets, until ruin overtakes them. For when the prophet is cast aside, there is no refuge but destruction. As it is written:

"Indeed, God does not wrong the people at all, but it is the people who wrong themselves" (Qur'an, Sūrat Yūnus سورة يونس *"Jonah" 10:44).*

The False Peace of Settled Urban Elites

They cannot bear the grace. The grace that unmasks their allegiance to what we term "the one percent." The settled urban elites. The people who love injustice. Grace is offered and refused. They chose Pharaoh's false peace. It is cowardice disguised as civility, an ancient flavor of "Minnesota nice."

In the end, they take no stand. And know: to take no stand is the most wicked stand of all. For they rejected the Messiah and turned aside from the Command. Yet they sit in their houses, feasting at their tables, smiling with one another, as though judgment will not overtake them.

Found Judgment: Divine Justice and Exposure

The Damocles Sword

The last example, because it is Scripture, represents judgment. The people "find" judgment, מ־צ־א (*mem-ṣade-aleph*). Not by seeking it but by standing in the way of divine mercy. Again, in Luke they witness the healed man. And do they respond with submission like Benjamin? No, they respond with fear. So, the grace that was shown to the man becomes an آية (*ayah*), a sign of wrath and judgment for those who reject it. The Arabic آية (*ayah*) indicates both "verse" and "sign," connecting textual and natural phenomena as divine proclamation.

This reversal echoes throughout Scripture. To find is not to find. It is to be found out by God, exposed, weighed, measured, and confronted. The finding unmasks guilt. And you can be certain that God's justice follows swiftly. It does not matter that grace has already been extended. That is why, for years, in the classroom, Fr. Paul Tarazi used the image of the Sword of Damocles to illustrate biblical grace: grace as the constant threat and danger that accompanies the power of God's judgment: the ever-present risk of betrayal, upheaval, or, for the prophets, death. It is an apt metaphor. To be found by God is double-edged. You cannot tempt him. You must not trifle with him.

Romanticized Justice

People are superficial. They romanticize justice but will not bear its weight. They will sell out their own brother in an instant for the sake of comfort. They admire the idea of justice for the poor, but not insofar as it requires what it demands of them. Such an assertion collapses under its own hypocrisy.

"We were fine in Egypt."

"Yes, it is truly sad what's happening in Gaza, but why do we have to keep talking about it?"

Such responses serve only to dodge serious reckoning. Again, the swine.

Egypt: Found Wanting

We return to the itinerary of the root in Genesis 47. Egypt is found wanting, stripped, bare. It is found powerless before God, lacking, emptied of silver, and reduced to servitude:

וַיְלַקֵּט יוֹסֵף אֶת־כָּל־הַכֶּסֶף הַנִּמְצָא בְאֶרֶץ־מִצְרַיִם וּבְאֶרֶץ־כְּנַעַן
בַּשֶּׁבֶר אֲשֶׁר־הֵם שֹׁבְרִים וַיָּבֵא יוֹסֵף אֶת־הַכֶּסֶף בֵּיתָה פַּרְעֹה

wayyeqqat yosef ʾet-kol-hakkesef hannimṣaʾ beʾereṣ miṣrayim ubeʾereṣ kenaʿan bašeber ʾašer hem šobrim wayyabeʾ yosef ʾet-hakkesef beytah farʿoh

"And Joseph gathered up all the money that was found in the land of Egypt and in the land of Canaan, in exchange for the grain that they bought" (Genesis 47:14)

A Thief Like Egypt

Empires have silver and food because they are thieves. And here in Exodus, a thief like Egypt is found in possession of stolen goods. And the act triggers justice:

אִם־הִמָּצֵא תִמָּצֵא בְיָדוֹ הַגְּנֵבָה מִשּׁוֹר עַד־חֲמוֹר עַד־שֶׂה חַיִּים
שְׁנַיִם יְשַׁלֵּם

ʾim-himmaseʾ timmaseʾ beyado hagenebah mišor ʿad-ḥamor ʿad-seh ḥayyim šenayim yešallem

"If the stolen beast is found alive in his possession, whether it is an ox or a donkey or a sheep, he shall pay double" (Exodus 22:4)

Found in Rebellion

The people gather manna on the Sabbath against God's command and are found in rebellion:

וַיְהִי בַּיּוֹם הַשְּׁבִיעִי יָצְאוּ מִן־הָעָם לִלְקֹט וְלֹא מָצָאוּ

wayehi bayyom hašbiʿi yaṣʾu min-haʿam lilqot weloʾ maṣaʾu

"On the seventh day some of the people went out to gather, but they found none" (Exodus 16:27)

They found nothing because they were disobedient. The prophet in Ezekiel searches for one righteous person in Jerusalem but finds no one:

וָאֲבַקֵּשׁ מֵהֶם אִישׁ גֹּדֵר־גָּדֵר וְעֹמֵד בַּפֶּרֶץ לְפָנַי בְּעַד הָאָרֶץ
לְבִלְתִּי שַׁחֲתָהּ וְלֹא מָצָאתִי

waʾabaqeš mehem ʾiš goder-gader weʿomed bafferef lefanay beʿad haʾareṣ lebilti šaḥatah weloʾ maṣaʾti

The Desert Knows His Name

> *"And I sought for a man among them who should build up the wall and stand in the breach before me for the land, that I should not destroy it, but I found none" (Ezekiel 22:30)*

No one.

The Trap of Discovery

To find is not mere discovery, but encounter. It is to stand exposed before the decree of the Almighty. In seeking, man uncovers only his own vanity, his own corruption: the emptiness woven into his being. What is found is not blessing but snare, not life but the sentence of his end.

The final verse exemplifies once more the functionality of מ־צ־א (*mem-ṣade-aleph*), now in its most severe form: judgment brought to completion, where all that is found is consigned to destruction. But destruction in Scripture is not annihilation, it is restoration. Woe to what men build, for it shall be undone. Woe to their towers, for they shall crumble. Woe to their cities, for they shall return to dust. Thus does the Lord strip away the works of human hands, that creation may be restored to the order in which he first ordained it. And you will be found naked again in the תּוֹלְדוֹת (*toledot*) of the heavens and the earth, standing with your elder brother, the fish, and your neighbor, the bear. You will dwell beneath the light of the moon and the stars, under the branch of the tree, beside the dove who finds rest in its shelter. Such is the decree of the Lord: He returns all things to their place, each to its measure, each to its dwelling, none forgotten, none spared, all restored.

Self-Inflicted Destruction

In Scripture, to find is never an innocent act; it is invariably bound to condemnation. This explains why the people do not rejoice when they behold the healed man in Luke 8: they recoil, for in him they encounter themselves. And in finding themselves, the face of their birth pronounces judgment.

The same functional pattern emerges in Judges 20 with the tribe of Benjamin. Note how the terminology interlocks: having already encountered Benjamin in connection with the planted cup of Genesis 44, we meet him again here. The linguistic thread of the root מ־צ־א (*mem-ṣade-aleph*) binds these episodes, tracing a coherent lexical itinerary across the parabolic fabric of Scripture. In Judges, Benjamin commits a grievous crime and is pursued by the other tribes. The plot culminates in devastation: every city that is found is destroyed, judgment executed through total annihilation.

וְאִישׁ יִשְׂרָאֵל שָׁבוּ אֶל־בְּנֵי בִנְיָמִן וַיַּכּוּם לְפִי־חֶרֶב מֵעִיר מְתֹם
עַד־בְּהֵמָה עַד כָּל־הַנִּמְצָא גַּם כָּל־הֶעָרִים הַנִּמְצָאוֹת שִׁלְּחוּ בָאֵשׁ

weʾîš yiṣraʾel šabu ʾel-bene binyamin wayyakkum lefi-ḥereb meʿir metom ʿad-behemah ʿad kol-hannimṣaʾ gam kol-heʿarim hannimṣaʾot šilleḥu baʾeš

"And the men of Israel turned back against the people of Benjamin and struck them with the edge of the sword, the city, men and beasts and all that they found. And all the towns that they found they set on fire" (Judges 20:48)

But here is the complexity: the destruction unfolds entirely on God's chessboard, so to speak. Yet what is striking is that the text never says God ordered it, and that matters. The violence is Israel's own doing. Is this divine justice, or human vengeance? Following the itinerary back to Genesis raises unsettling questions, for Benjamin had submitted. Something's happening here, as the song says, and "what it is ain't exactly clear."[52]

In this case, the burning of cities and the annihilation of everything found (הַנִּמְצָא, *hannimṣa'*) embodies the arrogance of civilization, of settled elites taking judgment into their own hands. Rather than accepting the judgment that restores, the people in Luke 8 invite the judgment that builds civilization at another's expense. Their nearness to God's justice, which they resist, turns grace into condemnation. This is the very mechanism at work in Luke 8:35-37.

Banū Naḍīr and Self-Destruction

Inter-functional Scripture

The Qur'an, in 59:2, follows this same pattern.[53] I have discussed this example previously, and it remains functional here. Terminologically, the Banū Naḍīr bring destruction upon themselves, not because God desires their ruin, but because they spurn his mercy:

هُوَ الَّذِي أَخْرَجَ الَّذِينَ كَفَرُوا مِنْ أَهْلِ الْكِتَابِ مِن دِيَارِهِمْ
لِأَوَّلِ الْحَشْرِ مَا ظَنَنْتُمْ أَن يَخْرُجُوا وَظَنُّوا أَنَّهُم مَّانِعَتُهُمْ
حُصُونُهُم مِّنَ اللهِ فَأَتَاهُمُ اللهُ مِنْ حَيْثُ لَمْ يَحْتَسِبُوا وَقَذَفَ

---

[52] Buffalo Springfield. *For What It's Worth.* Atco Records, 1967. The line "What it is ain't exactly clear" appears in the opening verse.

[53] Sūrat al-Hashr 59:2 describes the exile of the Banū Naḍīr tribe from Medina.

فِي قُلُوبِهِمُ الرُّعْبَ يُخْرِبُونَ بُيُوتَهُم بِأَيْدِيهِمْ وَأَيْدِي الْمُؤْمِنِينَ فَاعْتَبِرُوا يَا أُولِي الأَبْصَارِ

huwa alladhī akhraja alladhīna kafarū min ahli al-kitābi min diyārihim li-awwali al-ḥashri mā ẓanantum an yakhrujū wa-ẓannū annahum māniʿatuhum ḥuṣūnuhum mina allāhi fa-atāhumu allāhu min ḥaythu lam yaḥtasibū wa-qadhafa fī qulūbihimu ar-ruʿba yukhribūna buyūtahum bi-aydīhim wa-aydī al-muʾminīna fa-iʿtabirū yā ūlī al-abṣāri

"It is he who expelled those who disbelieved among the People of the Book from their homes at the first gathering. You did not think they would leave, and they thought that their fortresses would protect them from God; but God came upon them from where they had not expected, and he cast terror into their hearts [so] they destroyed their houses by their own hands and the hands of the believers. So, take warning, O people of vision" (Qur'an, Sūrat al-Ḥashr سورة الحشر *"The Exile" or "The Gathering" 59:2)*

Even when God does not explicitly command it, he remains the one in control. The same dynamic operates in the book of Judges. The Qur'an hears the Bible. They are inter-functional, bound together in one fabric of judgment. Here, destruction falls not only because of rebellion, but because the mercy inherent in divine judgment, once refused, is twisted into a pretext for power wielded by human principalities. What was given as grace becomes weaponized by human hands, and so judgment descends like the Sword of Damocles, ever suspended above the heads of those who resist his mercy with their own works.

The Double-Edged Surah

The brilliance of the scholars of al-Andalus, masters of both Arabic and Hebrew, lies in their attentiveness to the roots and their functions. For us, this is paramount. Take, for example, the title of Sūrat al-Ḥashr (سورة الحشر). The Arabic word حَشْر (*ḥashr*), derived from the triliteral root ح-ش-ر (*ḥāʾ-shīn-rāʾ*), conveys the sense of gathering, assembling, mustering; driving together, collecting, compelling into a group; and, by extension, exile or being driven out. Within a single term, the double-edged nature of divine action is inscribed. Here the intertextuality is unmistakable: in Luke, is it gathering or exile? Which is it, grace or judgment? The function itself bears what we might call the Tarazian Sword of Damocles: divine grace, ever double-edged: restoring the lost while scattering the proud.

Even the very title of the surah is Pauline, resonating with the language of Paul's epistles and Luke's gospel. The scandal of the Protestant Reformation is that Orientalists and Crusaders, in their arrogance, ignored the Arabic text, thus blinding themselves to this essential tension. Gathering or exile: this is the hinge of the Lukan parable! The mercy that restores the outcast and gathers the lost sheep is the same mercy that scatters the proud in the imagination of their hearts. As the Magnificat proclaims:

ἐποίησεν κράτος ἐν βραχίονι αὐτοῦ, διεσκόρπισεν ὑπερηφάνους διανοίᾳ καρδίας αὐτῶν

epoiesen kratos en brachioni autou dieskorpisen hyperphanous dianoia kardias autou

"He has shown strength with his arm; he has scattered the proud in the imagination of their hearts" (Luke 1:51)

Arabic Root Excavation: و-ج-د (*wāw-jīm-dāl*) as Divine Encounter

The Qur'anic Itinerary

To find, و-ج-د (*wāw-jīm-dāl*), the corresponding function in Arabic, is to find as judgment, as mercy, as unveiling. This is the Qur'anic itinerary of و-ج-د: as with Hebrew, to find is never mere discovery, but confrontation, an encounter between the human being and God's will. God, who is all-merciful and all-wise, grants either his mercy or his judgment. In the Qur'an, the usage of و-ج-د holds the biblical line, maintaining this reality of encounter and confrontation.

SŪRAT AL-ḌUḤĀ: GOD FINDS HIS SLAVE

In *Sūrat al-Ḍuḥā,* God finds his slave:

وَوَجَدَكَ ضَالًا فَهَدَىٰ

wa-wajadaka ḍāllan fa-hadā

"And he found you lost and guided [you]" (Qur'an, Sūrat al-Ḍuḥā سورة الضحى *"The Morning Hours" 93:7)*

Here, God finds Muḥammad lacking guidance and brings him under instruction. To be found is not discovery, it is confrontation. It is as Paul declared: "But now that you have come to know God, or rather to be known by God" (Galatians 4:9). You are not the reference; He is the reference, so that you hear and submit.

And Paul proclaimed redemption: "Christ redeemed (ἐξηγόρασεν, *exēgorasen*) us from the curse of the law" (Galatians 3:13), and again, "to redeem those who were under the law" (Galatians 4:5). Redemption is not earned; it is given: "We know that a man is declared righteous not (οὐ δικαιοῦται, *ou dikaioutai*) by works of the law but through trust in Jesus Christ" (Galatians 2:16).

You are a found man. Not found by the mob at Gerasa but by the Almighty. The referent is Jesus, the Son of the Father, not the people. You are found by God and rejected by men. Thus, it is written:

> *"The people went out to see what had happened; and they came to Jesus, and found the man from whom the demons had gone out, sitting down at the feet of Jesus, clothed and in his right mind; and they became frightened. Those who had seen it reported to them how the man who was demon-possessed had been made well. And all the people of the country of the Gerasenes and the surrounding district asked him to leave them, for they were gripped with great fear; and he got into a boat and returned." (Luke 8:35-37).*

This is the seal: to be found is to be judged, to be redeemed, to be cast out. He finds, he redeems, he casts down, he exalts. He is the reference, and there is no other. Who is like him?

Sūrat al-Nūr: The Mirage and Reckoning

Sūrat al-Nūr and a reckoning. And he finds God before him, and he fully pays him his due:

وَوَجَدَ اللّهَ عِندَهُ فَوَفَّاهُ حِسَابَهُ

wa-wajada allāha ʿindahu fa-waffāhu ḥisābahu

"But when he comes to it, he finds nothing but finds God before him, and he will pay him in full his due" (Qur'an, Sūrat al-Nūr سورة النور *"The Light" 24:39)*

This verse contrasts superficial appearance with divine fruit. It is the *ergon* (ἔργον) that God places in you, *his ergon*. For the one who does not believe, the deeds are a mirage: they seem impressive yet are empty. This is Paul's very definition of Satan, "who opposes and exalts himself against every so-called god or object of worship" and comes "with all power and false signs and wonders" (2 Thessalonians 2:4, 9). Paul himself uses the expression ἐν ἔργῳ (*en ergo*) in 1 Thessalonians 1:3, "your work of faith" (τοῦ ἔργου τῆς πίστεως, *tou ergou tes pisteos*), to describe the genuine fruit God alone produces, and forcefully, Philippians 2:13, the work God himself puts in you (θεὸς γάρ ἐστιν ὁ ἐνεργῶν ἐν ὑμῖν, *theos gar estin ho energon en hymin*), "for it is God who works in you", in stark contrast to the empty show of the adversary. When someone looks for God, in other words, the Greek, the Hellenist, the seeker, when someone "finds" God, it is not for mercy, but for judgment, for reckoning. As the Apostle Paul said:

"You do not know God but are known by him."
(Galatians 4:9)

To be found out is to stand exposed with no illusions, no mirage able to shield your deeds. This is the light النور *(al-nūr)* that shines in the darkness. (John 1:5):

τὸ φῶς ἐν τῇ σκοτίᾳ φαίνει, καὶ ἡ σκοτία αὐτὸ οὐ κατέλαβεν (John 1:5)

to phos en te skotia phainei, kai he skotia auto ou katelaben

"The light shines in the darkness, and the darkness has not overcome it"

Do you still intend to leave some of these books outside your library, as though the words of the Lord could be trimmed? Will you cut away what his hand has planted? Will you withhold what he has gathered? Do you imagine that by your erasure you can diminish his speech? Woe to the one who builds shelves for himself yet leaves out the scrolls of God. And now you erase even the little ones, just as you have erased his words. But the Day is near: "And your Lord comes, and the angels, rank upon rank." (Qur'an, Sūrat al-Fajr سورة الفجر "The Dawn" 89:22)

Sūrat al-Kahf: Moses Finds a Slave of God

فَوَجَدَا عَبْدًا مِّنْ عِبَادِنَا آتَيْنَاهُ رَحْمَةً مِّنْ عِندِنَا وَعَلَّمْنَاهُ مِن لَّدُنَّا عِلْمًا

fa-wajadā ʿabdan min ʿibādinā ātaynāhu raḥmatan min ʿindinā wa-ʿallamnāhu min ladunnā ʿilman

"And they found one of our slaves to whom we had given mercy from us and had taught him from us a [certain] knowledge" (Qur'an, Sūrat al-Kahf سورة الكهف *"The Cave" 18:65)*

Moses, a major figure in the Qur'an, sought a deeper understanding of the Torah and found a slave of God, traditionally identified as al-Khiḍr. This figure imparts divine wisdom to Moses through actions that are scandalous and unsettling. In this mashal, to "find" is to be confronted with God's wisdom, which is not man's wisdom. It is the wisdom of the Abrahmic scrolls, God's wisdom, that defies human reason, overturns the moral calculations of Greek ethics, and exposes the inadequacy of Roman law:

> *"'For my thoughts are not your thoughts, nor are your ways my ways,' declares the Lord. 'For as the heavens are higher than the earth, so are my ways higher than your ways and my thoughts than your thoughts.'" (Isaiah 55:8-9)*

The conduct of this slave shakes the foundations of human judgment. Moses, for a moment swayed by the glitter of Hellenistic ideals of justice—those same ideals that Crusaders and Greco-Romans now parade under the banner of "Judeo-Christianism"—is humbled by al-Khiḍr, the slave who moves only under divine command. His very name, al-Khiḍr (الخضر), "the Green One," speaks of hidden life, of renewal, of a vitality unseen. Yet more plainly still, his name recalls the primordial garden, the dwelling of Genesis, before it was spoiled by Greco-Roman tyranny. And so, I ask you again: will you persist in defending your amputated libraries?

Elijah Not Found, Yet Fed

Hidden from Kings and False Judgments

There is one final example of this root's itinerary that I wish to emphasize, and it is decisive. Elijah was not found. This is technical. "But when they searched for him, they could not find him" (2 Kings 2:17). This sets the paradigm for the righteous who escape being "found" by the hands of men. He was not found, yet he was fed by עֲרָבִים (*'arabim*), nomadic pastoral tribes, Arabs,[54] ravens. The term itself signifies a mingling, an interwoven people who move beneath the moonlight: Bedouins, like birds, hidden from the courts of kings and beyond the judgments of men.

The Qur'an, too, remembers Elijah, bearing witness to him among the righteous, hidden and preserved: "And indeed, Elijah was among the messengers" (Qur'an, Sūrat al-Ṣāffāt سورة الصافات "Those Who Set the Ranks" 37:123-132). The intertext is unmistakable. Both traditions preserve the same functionality: the prophet unseen, unfound by human judgment, sustained only by the mercy of God.

As it is written:

> זַרְעוֹ לְעוֹלָם יִהְיֶה וְכִסְאוֹ כַשֶּׁמֶשׁ נֶגְדִּי כְּיָרֵחַ יִכּוֹן עוֹלָם וְעֵד
> בַּשַּׁחַק נֶאֱמָן

---

[54] Salibi, Kamal S., *The Bible Came from Arabia* (London: Jonathan Cape, 1985), esp. the genealogical and linguistic chapters re-examining Hebrew terms in light of Arabic parallels; see also The Pulpit Commentary on 1 Kings 17:4-6, noting that the Hebrew word for "ravens" may alternatively be read as "Arabians" (Com. Eds. Spence-Jones, 1909).

zar'o le'olam yihyeh wekhiso kašameš negdi kayyareah yikon 'olam we'ed baššahaq ne'eman

"His offspring shall endure forever, his throne as long as the sun before me. Like the moon it shall be established forever, a faithful witness in the skies" (Psalm 89:36-37)

تَبَارَكَ الَّذِي جَعَلَ فِي السَّمَاءِ بُرُوجًا وَجَعَلَ فِيهَا سِرَاجًا وَقَمَرًا مُّنِيرًا

tabāraka alladhī ja'ala fī as-samā'i burūjan wa-ja'ala fīhā sirājan wa-qamaran munīran

"Blessed is he who has placed in the sky great stars and placed therein a [burning] lamp and luminous moon" (Qur'an, Sūrat al-Furqān سورة الفرقان *"The Criterion" 25:61)*

Jesus and Elijah: Not Found Among the Condemned

The New Testament identifies Jesus with Elijah. Like Elijah, Jesus was not found among the condemned, for he was justified by God and raised in power against the ruler of this world. This identification recurs throughout the gospels. As it is written:

וַיֵּלְכוּ וַיְבַקְשֻׁהוּ שְׁלֹשָׁה יָמִים וְלֹא מְצָאֻהוּ

wayyelku wayebaqšuhu šelošah yamim welo' meṣa'uhu

"They went and sought him for three days but did not find him" (2 Kings 2:17)

The Desert Knows His Name

The righteous are not found because they are not condemned. This is the final reversal of the מ־צ־א (*mem-ṣade-ʾaleph*) functionality: those who are righteous elude human "finding" precisely because they have already been found by God. The human search fails not due to divine absence but because divine protection conceals them. Hidden in God, the righteous stand beyond the reach of human judgment and imperial power.

Implications

The mechanisms in Luke 8:35-37 remain active today. The people of Gerasa, who found the healed man and responded with fear instead of joy, embody a recurring human pattern: when divine mercy dismantles our systems of control, we prefer the false peace of empire to the unsettling grace of God's kingdom. Such grace unmasks allegiance to settled elites who thrive on injustice.

Everything found is double-edged. Grace if received, judgment if refused. The light of instruction burns, and those who find must beware. Today, political and religious leaders still invoke biblical authority to defend the very systems Scripture opposes: imperial harlotry that cloaks rebellion against God in biblical language.

The wound of the House of Trastámara, first heirs of the Crusader legacy, still festers. The exclusion of Arabic wisdom from biblical studies is no mere oversight but a willful amputation of a primary linguistic tradition. The scholars of al-Andalus showed what is possible when the sons of Noah labor together under the tent of shared textual study, focusing on roots over translations, function over interpretation.

The mercy that restores the outcast also scatters the proud. Those who find divine favor stand in the breach; those who meet mercy with fear condemn themselves. Luke's account is not simply a local exorcism but a confrontation between divine and human authority. The people must choose: submit like Benjamin or shrink back into the safety of slavery.

As Paul taught, there is no God but one. We do not know him; we are known by him. The reference point is not our seeking but his finding. We are found by the Almighty, not by our own enlightenment. No longer seeking to be central, our task becomes patient, faithful work: tracing roots, recording usage, transmitting what we find, trusting that God has spoken.

Finders, beware: in Scripture, finding often signals the onset of divine action, never good news from a human point of view. Yet for those who submit rather than resist, who stand firm rather than flee to Egypt, finding becomes grace. The desert knows his name, and in that knowing we are found.

Incense and Ash

The function ש־ו־ב (*šin-waw-bet)* is not the sigh of remorse in a cloistered heart, but the pivot of a sword's edge; the turn God commands into the place where his name has been denied. Abraham returns from the valley of kings; Moses returns to the mountain, still breathing the smoke of the calf's golden stench; Gideon returns to the camp with the dream of victory burning in his ears. None turns to hide. All turn to face him.

And ח־נ־ן (*ḥet-nun-nun*), to plead, is no bowing before the courts of men. The human reference vanishes. Job's feeble plea to his servant falls into the void. Malachi mocks the lips that beg for favor while the hands bring defilement. Proper pleading is stripped of flattery and calculation, bare as incense in the wind, carrying no name but his.

In Luke's Gerasene plain, the return is marked by absence. The swine are gone, the crowd is gone, the man's former companions erased. He stands alone, clothed and found, with no community left to shield him, no filth left to hide him, no power left to reference but the one who sent him. This is the Day when the disbeliever is given back his own deed, when tribe and city and oath are dust, and a man stands naked before the Face that made him.

This is the Day that the Lord has made.

To return is to step into that bareness now, ahead of the Hour, with only obedience in your hands.

Return to your house, Ḥabibi, and describe what great things God has done for you.

The Return to Contested Territory: A Detheological Analysis of Luke 8:39

The Grammar of Prophetic Confrontation

The commission Jesus gives to the healed Gerasene has been psychologized by centuries of therapeutic interpretation that reduces divine command to personal spirituality, the narcissistic obsession with inner healing and self-discovery that evades the text's demand for duty toward God. What matters is not what people want or how they feel, but what God commands. Scripture is not about personal piety but about being cornered with what you are and submitting to divine authority, not the sentimental rehabilitation fantasies of spiritual directors who mistake prophetic confrontation for psychological counseling about personal testimony, relationship, and community. Indeed, when we excavate the terminological bedrock of Luke 8:39 through the triliteral root methodology of al-Andalus, a radically different picture emerges. The Greek ὑποστρέφω (*hypostrepho*, "to return") activates the Hebrew ש-ו-ב (*šin-waw-bet*) and its Arabic cognate ث-و-ب (*thāʾ-wāw-bāʾ*), revealing a semantic field that consistently signifies not pietistic retreat but strategic advance into contested territory, the prophetic return that confronts rather than accommodates.[55]

[55] The Hebrew root ש־ו־ב (*šin-waw-bet*) means "to return, to turn back," a Semitic imperative grounded in covenantal obedience. In the Septuagint, it is often rendered as μετάνοια (*metanoia*), yet the distortion lies not in this correspondence but in later theology, which reimagined μετάνοια as an interior "change of mind." This

The Lexicographical Foundation: Beyond Theological Domestication

The persistent mistranslation of ש-ו-ב as "repentance" in theological discourse represents a fundamental misunderstanding of its biblical function. Contemporary scholarship, trapped within Greco-Roman interpretive frameworks, reduces this dynamic root to internal psychological categories that obscure its martial and confrontational character. Yet the lexicographical

---

abstraction betrays the consonantal force of ש־ו־ב, which must be heard across the breadth of its usages in the Hebrew text itself, not through the lens of the Greek (pagan) imagination. Within Scripture, ש־ו־ב resounds in parable, command, and prophetic utterance alike, demanding concrete action: the people must return to Torah, to the path from which they have strayed. To filter this root through philosophical categories is to sever it from its scriptural itinerary, replacing obedience with introspection. In the tradition of al-Andalus, where Jewish and Muslim scholars pursued the consonantal roots across Hebrew and Arabic alike, the integrity of ש־ו־ב is preserved. It is not a speculative concept to be systematized but a command that resounds again and again in the text: return!

In fact, in the Septuagint, ש־ו־ב is not confined to μετάνοια but corresponds to a constellation of Greek verbs that preserve its concrete sense of turning or returning. These include ἐπιστρέφω (*epistrepho*), "to turn back, to return," often used for Israel's return to the Lord (Isaiah 55:7; Jerermiah 3:12); ἀναστρέφω (*anastrepho*), "to turn about, to conduct oneself," expressing behavior; ἀποστρέφω (*apostrepho*), "to turn away," underscoring refusal or rejection; and μεταστρέφω (*metastrepho*), "to turn around, to change," highlighting reversal of direction. This semantic range shows that the translators themselves retained the concrete itinerary of ש־ו־ב, while theology reduced it to interiority, objectifying μετάνοια as though it were a Platonic form. In so doing, theology erased the consonantal richness of ש־ו־ב, whose scriptural usage makes clear that repentance is not a shift of thought but a deed, a covenantal return, often into the fray, as an act of submission.

evidence across Hebrew, Arabic, and Greek usage demonstrates that "return" in scriptural contexts signifies tactical reengagement, not withdrawal.

The Archaeological Excavation of δέομαι (*deomai*) / ח־נ־ן (*ḥet-nun-nun*) / ح-ن-ن (*ḥāʾ-nūn-nūn*)

> *Luke 8:38: παρεκάλει δὲ αὐτὸν ὁ ἀνὴρ ἀφ' οὗ ἐξεληλύθει τὰ δαιμόνια εἶναι σὺν αὐτῷ*
>
> *"But the man from whom the demons had gone out was begging [παρεκάλει (*parekalei*)] him that he might accompany him."*

The Greek δέομαι (*deomai*) and παρακαλέω (*parakaleo*) correspond to the Hebrew ח־נ־ן (*ḥanan*), which in biblical usage denotes not generic pleading but orientation toward correct authority. This term corresponds to נָחַם (*naḥam*) in the canonical consonantal Hebrew text, and in Arabic to the root ح-ن-ن (*ḥāʾ-nūn-nūn*).

To plead is no bowing before the courts of men. Proper pleading is stripped of flattery and calculation, bare as incense in the wind, carrying no name but his. The question is not the act of pleading but the direction of the plea: the reference point that determines whether the petition ascends as incense or descends as stench.

The Itinerary of ח־נ־ן: From Divine Entreaty to Imperial Corruption

The itinerary of ח־נ־ן opens with righteous entreaty to God in Deuteronomy 3:23:

וָאֶתְחַנַּן אֶל־יְהוָה בָּעֵת הַהִוא לֵאמֹר

wa'ethannan 'el-yahweh ba'et hahiw le'mor

*"I pleaded [*וָאֶתְחַנַּן *(*wa'etḥannan*)] with the Lord at that time"*

Here Moses petitions the Lord to let him cross the Jordan and view the promised land. The verb, drawn from the root ח־נ־ן (*ḥet-nun-nun*), frames his request not as a demand but as a plea for unmerited grace. This establishes the proper reference point for Israel: direct appeal to divine authority, acknowledging that entry into the land, like all covenantal gifts, depends entirely upon God's mercy, not human claim. The itinerary proceeds to submission before divine authority through prophetic representation in 2 Kings 1:13:

וַיִּתְחַנֵּן אֵלָיו וַיְדַבֵּר אֵלָיו אִישׁ הָאֱלֹהִים יִֽקַר־נָא נַפְשִׁי וְנֶפֶשׁ עֲבָדֶיךָ אֵלֶּה חֲמִשִּׁים בְּעֵינֶיךָ

wayyithannen 'elayw wayyedabber 'elayw 'iš ha'elohim yiqqar-na' nafši wenefeš 'abdeka 'elleh hamiššim be'eyneka

*"he bowed down on his knees before Elijah and begged [*וַיִּתְחַנֵּן *(*wayyitḥannen*)] him"*

This act of submission before Elijah demonstrates the same pattern: entreaty for favor is directed not to human personality but to the function of divine authority operating through God's appointed slave. The posture is one of submission: a functional recognition of the prophet as God's *locum tenens.* It is neither ideological nor an ontological elevation of the human person, but at the same time, it is indeed personal, in the sense that an individual stands out temporarily, as Paul says, "an earthen vessel," (2 Corinthians 4:7) in the exercise of God's permenent power.

Job's Misdirected Appeal and the Corruption of Reference

ח־נ־ן (*ḥet-nun-nun*) is upheld as the correct course in Job 8:5:

אִם־אַתָּה תְּשַׁחֵר אֶל־אֵל וְאֶל־שַׁדַּי תִּתְחַנָּן

ʾim-ʾatta tešḥar ʾel-ʾel weʾel-šadday titḥannan

*"if you will search for God and implore [*תִּתְחַנָּן *(*titḥannan*)] the compassion of the Almighty"*

Here the course is clear: entreaty for favor must be directed to God alone. Job is held up as correct on the condition he will seek and implore the compassion of the Almighty. Yet there is always a fly in the ointment with this character, for he embodies the self-serving fascistic justice that men project onto Scripture.

Thus, in Job 19:16 the function falters:

לְעַבְדִּי קָרָאתִי וְלֹא יַעֲנֶה בְּמוֹ־פִי אֶתְחַנֶּן־לוֹ

leʿabdi qaraʾti weloʾ yaʿaneh bemo-fi ʾetḥannen-lo

*"I called to my slave, but he gave me no answer; I pleaded [*אֶתְחַנֶּן *(ʾ*etḥannen*)] with him with my mouth."*

Why do you pray to a human being? You fool. This is the verbal equivalent of being found in the wrong place: misoriented, exposed, powerless. Job is found out in his misdirected appeal. The form of prayer remains, but its object is corrupted. The text lays bare that even correct prayer is worthless if the one who pleads is corrupt.

The Prophetic Critique: Malachi's Final Word

The itinerary of ח־נ־ן (*ḥet-nun-nun*) terminates in Malachi 1:9:

> וְעַתָּה חַלּוּ־נָא פְנֵי־אֵל וִיחָנֵנוּ מִיֶּדְכֶם הָיְתָה־זֹּאת הֲיִשָּׂא מִכֶּם פָּנִים אָמַר יְהוָה צְבָאוֹת

> *we'attah ḥallu-na' fenei-'el wiyḥanenu miyyedkem hayetah-zot hayissa mikem fanim amar yahweh ṣeba'ot*

> *"will you not plead [*חַלּוּ *(*ḥallu*)] for God's favor...with such an offering...will he receive any of you kindly?"*

Here the prophet exposes the futility, the sheer vanity, of petition without obedience. The work of defiled hands produces stench in God's nostrils, not incense. This is technical in the prophets: a persistent critique throughout the Hebrew Bible that sacrifice, worship, and ritual are nothing if the hands that offer them are unclean. "An abomination" in Isaiah (1:13), rejected along with festivals and assemblies in Amos (5:21-23), and dismissed as worthless in Jeremiah (6:20) when severed from justice and obedience. Indeed, who then can pray? Malachi thereby seals the itinerary of ח־נ־ן (*ḥet-nun-nun*): the plea for grace is always possible, but its efficacy is voided when the petitioner himself stands condemned.

The Archaeological Excavation of ὑποστρέφω (*hypostrepho*) / ש־ו־ב (*šin-waw-bet*) / ث-و-ب (*thā'-wāw-bā'*)

The root ש־ו־ב (*šin-waw-bet*) is systematically mistranslated as "repentance" in theological discourse, reducing martial vocabulary to psychological categories. This mistranslation represents one of the most significant terminological corruptions in Western biblical interpretation. In the prophetic arc, ש־ו־ב (*šin-waw-bet*) does not denote an internal psychological shift but a strategic turn, a pivot of direction toward confrontation. Such a turn is rarely safe; it signals the peril of returning to God's path in defiance of entrenched powers, often leading directly into conflict, danger, and judgment. To hear ש־ו־ב (*šin-waw-bet*) through the lens of psychology is to domesticate its force; to hear it consonantally is to face the tactical, even martial, character of its demand: turn, and risk confrontation.

Against Therapeutic Repentance: The Military Topology of ث-و-ب / ש־ו־ב

The terminology associated with ש־ו־ב (*šin-waw-bet*) is consistently confrontational in character. To recover this usage is to expose the inadequacy of later theological renderings that psychologize the root into categories of individualized "repentance." Such interpretations reflect the pietistic and institutional domestication of the biblical text, reducing covenantal obedience to interior sentiment. In contrast, the prophetic deployment of ש־ו־ב (*šin-waw-bet*) conveys the language of strategic maneuver: a pivot, reversal, or repositioning that regularly entails confrontation with hostile human forces political, military, tribal, and institutional in nature, but always idolatrous. To abstract this vocabulary into a private, psychological, theraputic domain is a tactic characteristic of empire, a form of propaganda and distraction designed to obscure the Bible's original force and pedagogical function. The text was given to recall Israel from folly back to the perilous wisdom of submission and obedience, a wisdom that alone has the capacity to tear down the civlilizational cycles of human error and futility.

The Biblical Itinerary of Confrontational Return

Abraham: Strategic Reentry After Victory (Genesis 14:17)

אַחֲרֵי שׁוּבוֹ מֵהַכּוֹת אֶת־כְּדָרְלָעֹמֶר וְאֶת־הַמְּלָכִים אֲשֶׁר אִתּוֹ
וַיֵּצֵא מֶלֶךְ־סְדֹם לִקְרָאתוֹ אֶל־עֵמֶק שָׁוֵה הוּא עֵמֶק הַמֶּלֶךְ

ʾaḥarei šubo mehakot ʾet-kedarlaʿomer weʾet-hammelakim ʾašer ʾitto wayyetṣeʾ melek-sedom liqraʾto ʾel-ʿemeq šaweh huʾ ʿemeq hammelek

*"Then after his return [*שׁוּבוֹ *(*šubo*)] from the defeat of Chedorlaomer and the kings who were with him, the king of Sodom went out to meet him at the Valley of Shaveh (that is, the King's Valley)."*

Abraham's return ש־ו־ב (*šin-waw-bet*) from battle is not a triumphant homecoming but a strategic reentry into contested space. His return from victory leads directly into confrontation with the king of Sodom, a confrontation not of arms but of competing claims to authority. Abraham's posture is tactical: he places his trust not in the spoils of war or the favor of kings but in the Lord who delivered the enemy into his hands. ש־ו־ב (*šin-waw-bet*) here signals the next maneuver in a continuing conflict. The pivot of return is not rest but repositioning, an obedience that prepares Abraham to resist corrupt offers (Genesis 14:21-23) and affirm the Lord as sole benefactor.

EHUD: ASSASSINATION AS RETURN (JUDGES 3:19)

וְה֣וּא שָׁ֗ב מִן־הַפְּסִילִים֙ אֲשֶׁ֣ר אֶת־הַגִּלְגָּ֔ל וַיֹּ֕אמֶר דְּבַר־סֵ֥תֶר לִ֛י
אֵלֶ֖יךָ הַמֶּ֑לֶךְ וַיֹּ֣אמֶר הָ֔ס וַיֵּֽצְא֣וּ מֵעָלָ֔יו כָּל־הָעֹמְדִ֖ים עָלָֽיו

wehu' šab min-hafsilim 'ašer 'et-haggilgal wayyomer debar-seter li 'eileka hammelek wayyomer has wayyetse'u me'alayw kol-ha'omdim 'alayw

*"But he himself turned back [*שָׁב *(*šab*)] from the idols which were at Gilgal, and said, 'I have a secret message for you, O king.' And he said, 'Silence!' And all who were attending him left him."*

Here Ehud's ש־ו־ב (*šin-waw-bet*) is not penitence but strategy: a calculated turn back that sets the stage for assassination. The act of return functions as tactical misdirection. Appearing as retreat, it conceals the preparation for attack. In this way, ש־ו־ב (*šin-waw-bet*) manifests its military character: the pivot that transforms apparent withdrawal into decisive strike. The text unmasks the term's true register: not interior reflection but martial cunning, a maneuver that turns the tide of conflict.

Moses: Return to Face Divine Wrath (Exodus 32:31)

וַיָּשָׁב מֹשֶׁה אֶל־יְהוָה וַיֹּאמַר אָנָּא חָטָא הָעָם הַזֶּה חֲטָאָה גְדֹלָה
וַיַּעֲשׂוּ לָהֶם אֱלֹהֵי זָהָב

wayyašab moše ʾel-yahweh wayyomar ʾanna ḥata haʿam hazzeh ḥataʾah gedolah wayyaʿasu lahem ʾelohei zahab

*"Then Moses returned [*וַיָּשָׁב *(*wayyašab*)] to the Lord, and said, 'Oh, this people has committed a great sin, and they have made a god of gold for themselves!'"*

Moses's ש־ו־ב (*šin-waw-bet*) comes only after smashing the tablets, descending into the camp, and confronting Israel in their idolatry. His return is not a retreat but a perilous reentry into the sphere of divine wrath, carrying with him the stench of the golden calf's smoke. This is prophetic return at its most dangerous: Moses places himself in the breach between God and the people, standing as intercessor before judgment. Here ש־ו־ב (*šin-waw-bet*) signals not psychological contrition but tactical exposure: the prophet's hazardous pivot back into God's presence on behalf of a rebellious nation.

Gideon: Return to Rally the Faithful (Judges 7:15)

וַיְהִי כִשְׁמֹעַ גִּדְעוֹן אֶת־מִסְפַּר הַחֲלוֹם וְאֶת־שִׁבְרוֹ וַיִּשְׁתָּחוּ וַיָּשָׁב
אֶל־מַחֲנֵה יִשְׂרָאֵל וַיֹּאמֶר קוּמוּ כִּי־נָתַן יְהוָה בְּיֶדְכֶם אֶת־מַחֲנֵה
מִדְיָן

wayehi kišmoʿ gideʿon ʾet-misfar hallaḥalom weʾet-šibro wayyištahu wayyašab ʾel-maḥaneh yiṣraʾel wayyomer qumu ki-natan yahweh beyedkem ʾet-maḥaneh midyan

> *"When Gideon heard the account of the dream and its interpretation, he bowed in worship. Then he returned [*וַיָּשָׁב *(*wayyašab*)] to the camp of Israel and said, 'Arise, for the Lord has handed over to you the camp of Midian!'"*

Gideon's ש־ו־ב (*šin-waw-bet*) is a tactical pivot: he returns not to rest but to rally. Having overheard the enemy's dream of defeat, he bows before the Lord, then reenters the camp ablaze with conviction. His return is the turning point in the story, igniting faith in a mere three hundred men for one of the most audacious night operations in biblical mashal. Here, ש־ו־ב (*šin-waw-bet*) functions as the signal for action: the return of the leader galvanizes the troops for confrontation.

SAMSON: RETURN TO CONFRONTATION (JUDGES 14:8)

וַיָּשָׁב מִיָּמִים לְקַחְתָּהּ וַיָּסַר לִרְאוֹת אֵת מַפֶּלֶת הָאַרְיֵה וְהִנֵּה עֲדַת דְּבוֹרִים בִּגְוִיַּת הָאַרְיֵה וּדְבָשׁ

> *wayyašab miyamim leqaḥtah wayyasar lir'ot 'et-mafelet ha'aryeh wehinnah 'adat debarim bigwiyyat ha'aryeh udbaš*

> *"When he returned later [*וַיָּשָׁב *(*wayyašab*)] to take her, he turned aside to look at the carcass of the lion; and behold, a swarm of bees and honey were in the body of the lion."*

Once again, Samson's ש־ו־ב (*šin-waw-bet*) to Timnah is not neutral movement but a return laden with confrontation. He is drawn back to the site of his earlier kill, where death has become a riddle: sweetness issuing from decay. This return anticipates the conflict of the wedding feast, where the riddle of the honey becomes the spark for bloodshed (Judges 14:12-20). The detail of the swarm (עֲדַת דְּבוֹרִים, *'adat deborim*) heightens the irony. The term plays on the root ע־ד־ה (*'ayin-dalet-he*), which elsewhere denotes the assembly or congregation of Israel. Here it is grotesquely inverted: not God's people gathered under a *shepherd-of-flock*, but insects clustering around carrion. What should be a covenantal assembly has degenerated into a swarm circling death, in effect, a parody of obedience.

This same irony surfaces in Luke. In the synagogue at Nazareth (Luke 4:16-30), the συναγωγή (*synagoge*, "assembly") outwardly gathers as God's people but in function reveals itself as false עֵדָה (*'edah*) when it rejects Jesus as shepherd. Later, in the region of Gerasa (Luke 8:26-39), the crowd likewise rejects him after he confronts the unclean spirits. Instead of receiving the one who brings Torah, they beg him to depart. And yet, Jesus sends the healed man back to them. Not to retreat but to stand in confrontation, embodying the true Shepherd's authority against the false assembly.

In both cases, what appears to be congregation is exposed as swarm. The biblical text unmasks assemblies that refuse the Shepherd as nothing more than mobs clustering around death. Samson's return thus exposes the ambiguity of his calling: he is set apart as deliverer, yet his path loops through death, feasting, and confrontation. ש־ו־ב (*šin-waw-bet*) here is not a safe homecoming but a movement back into the perilous theater of conflict, where even sweetness is born of corruption.

*Paul's Blueprint: ὑποστρέφω (*hypostrepho*) as Apostolic Strategy*

Throughout Luke-Acts, the Greek ὑποστρέφω (*hypostrepho*) functions as the lexical blueprint for New Testament mission. Its definitional weight comes from its programmatic use in Paul's account in Galatians 1:17:

οὐδὲ ἀνῆλθον εἰς Ἱεροσόλυμα πρὸς τοὺς πρὸ ἐμοῦ ἀποστόλους, ἀλλὰ ἀπῆλθον εἰς Ἀραβίαν, καὶ πάλιν ὑπέστρεψα εἰς Δαμασκόν

oude anelthon eis Hierosolyma pros tous pro emou apostolous, alla apelthon eis Arabian, kai palin hypestrepsa eis Damaskon

*"nor did I go up to Jerusalem to those who were apostles before me; but I went away to Arabia, and returned again [ὑπέστρεψα (*hypestrepsa*)] to Damascus."*

Here the "return" is not an incidental travel detail but the strategic pivot of Paul's apostolic trajectory. His reentry into Damascus is laden with confrontation: he returns to the very synagogues that had once empowered him to persecute believers, now standing before them as رَسُولُ ٱللَّٰهِ (*rasūlu 'llāh*), the Messenger of God through Jesus Christ. This is ש־ו־ב (*šin-waw-bet*) in its prophetic function: not psychological repentance but reconfrontation with the seat of human resistance. In Paul's usage, ש־ו־ב (*šin-waw-bet*) is the perilous pivot back into hostile territory based on the divine commission that defines apostolic mission.

ACTS 13:13: CONFRONTING JEWISH LEADERSHIP

Paul and Barnabas, having completed their work in Cyprus, return (ὑποστρέφω, *hypostrepho*) to the synagogues of Antioch. Paul steps again into the very halls where he had once been sanctioned, now to proclaim the fulfillment of God's promise. His words cut both ways: they provoke opposition from those who will not yield, and they stir trust in those who recognize the voice of the Shepherd. This is the Abrahamic return: not to claim spoils, but to declare God's victory in the hearing of those who resist it.

ACTS 15:36: STRATEGIC CIRCUIT THROUGH CONTESTED TERRITORY

Later Paul proposes to Barnabas that they should return (ὑποστρέφω, *hypostrepho*) to every city where the words of God have been proclaimed. This is not a farewell tour but a strategic circuit. It is a deliberate reentry into contested territory to face down whatever opposition remains. Like Gideon returning to his camp after hearing the dream of Midian's defeat (Judges 7:15), Paul moves with quiet certainty that the battle is already decided, though the ground still needs to be claimed. His return is no closure but renewed confrontation, the tactical persistence that defines apostolic obedience.

The Qur'anic Correspondence: Divine Justice and Ultimate Return

ث-و-ب and the Return of Consequences

The Arabic triliteral root ث-و-ب (*thāʾ-wāw-bāʾ*) carries the same prophetic weight. To "return" in Qur'anic usage is not a neutral circling back but a summons to the very ground of risk, the place where fate and obedience are exposed. This arc reaches its sharpest edge in the final confrontation of the Day of Judgment, when the disbelievers are given back in full what they once dealt out (Qur'an, Sūrat al-Muṭaffifīn سورة المطفّفين "The Defrauders" or "Those Who Shortchange" 83:36). Here ثُوِّبَ (*thuwwiba*) marks the reentry of deeds upon their doers: divine justice returning action to its source, closing the circle of confrontation. Sūrat al-Muṭaffifīn 83:36:

هَلْ ثُوِّبَ ٱلْكُفَّارُ مَا كَانُوا يَفْعَلُونَ

hal thuwwiba l-kufāru mā kānū yafʿalūn

*"Have the disbelievers not been repaid [*ثُوِّبَ *(*thuwwiba*)] for what they used to do?"*

Here ثُوِّبَ (*thuwwiba*) marks the inevitable return of deeds upon their doers, a repayment that is less transaction than confrontation. What one has sown reenters one's own life as judgment. The return is not on the offender's terms but on God's terms, underscoring that divine justice is not a negotiation but a reckoning. As with ש־ו־ב (*šin-waw-bet*) in the Hebrew Bible and ὑποστρέφω (*hypostrepho*) in Luke-Acts, the Qur'anic usage situates "return" not in psychology but in the concrete arena of consequence, where human action circles back in divine response. This is the Day when the disbeliever is given back his own deed.

Paul's Return as Prophetic Anticipation

Paul's own ὑποστρέφω (*hypostrepho*) follows the prophetic itinerary of שׁ־ו־ב (*šin-waw-bet*): after withdrawing into Arabia, he returns to Damascus, the very city whose synagogues had once empowered his persecution of God's people. In that return, he reenters as the doer of his deeds, anticipating the judgment that will expose every work. His reentry is confrontation and testimony: he now stands as witness against the powers he once served, proclaiming the vindication of Jesus Christ, whom he now names Lord.

This return is not the desperate maneuver of a fugitive but the steady stride of one who knows the battle is already won. Paul does not return as a supplicant but as emissary of the victorious King, stepping onto ground secured by divine decree. Because the victory is God's, Paul has no need to vindicate himself. He can move with composure, even mercy, knowing the city is already his Master's. History later echoes this posture in Ṣalāḥ ad-Dīn's reentry into Jerusalem: triumph marked not by vengeance but by restraint, not by spectacle but by the quiet possession of what God had already promised.

Thus, Paul's ὑποστρέφω (*hypostrepho*) is both present defiance and future fidelity, a prophetic anticipation of judgment. His turning embodies alignment with the one revealed as Judge, when the kingdom is delivered up and the last enemy to be destroyed is death itself (1 Corinthians 15:24-26). In this sense, ὑποστρέφω (*hypostrepho*) carries the same force as שׁ־ו־ב (*šub*) and ثُوِّبَ (*thuwwiba*): the perilous pivot into confrontation that unmasks human and institutional resistance while anticipating the final reckoning.

This is the Sword of the Spirit, the sword wielded by God's Messenger, his Holy Apostle. The function אֵת (*ʾēt*, "plowshare") traces a brief but decisive itinerary in Scripture, appearing only five times.[56] It stands as the sign of God's righteous sword over the nations. First, in 1 Samuel (13:20-21) it marks Israel's subjugation. In Isaiah (2:4) it heralds the promise that Torah from Zion will transform violence into peace as swords beaten into plowshares. In Micah (4:3) it bears the covenantal function of agrarian security, a sign of restored life. Both texts echo the ancient Mesopotamian pattern of debt-forgiveness, which the Greco-Roman order would later suppress with its unforgiving morality codes.[57] Yet in

---

[56] The noun *ʾēt* (אֵת, "plowshare"), from the triliteral root א־ת־ת (*ʾalef-taw-taw*), is not the same as the common particle *ʾet* (אֶת) that marks the definite direct object. As a particle, *ʾet* (את) is a pointer word that shows what the action is happening to, like an arrow stating "this is the thing affected." For example, in "he took *ʾet* (את) the book," the word *ʾet* (את) doesn't indicate anything by itself; it simply points to the book as the object of the action. In the Hebrew consonantal text, *ʾet* (את) is a pointer when it stands before a definite object and never changes form, but it functions as "plowshare" when it behaves like a normal noun that can change, as in *ʾetim* (אֵתִים, "plowshares") or *le ʾetim* (לְאֵתִים, "into plowshares").

[57] Cooper, Matthew Franklin. *In the Houses of the Poor.* (St. Paul, MN: OCABS Press, 2025) p. 216. "… Again, this image is offered as comfort and encouragement (Apoc 1:4-7) to people who were faced with public mockery, torture, exile and death as a result of their opposition to Caesar and their support for the debt-relief program and jubilee politics which are shown in the Book of Acts." The human order, bound by law, morality, and the logic of wealth, can only tighten its grip. It defines righteousness by obedience to rules that preserve privilege. But God's order is reversal: release for the debtor, freedom for the slave, inheritance for the dispossessed.

Joel (4:10), the function is reversed: plowshares hammered back into swords, not for royal conquest but for divine ruin. Here the prophetic word collapses the myth of human progress as judgment falls, and even the tools of peace are re-forged as weapons of wrath.

In this way the root fulfills Jerusalem's lament: her suffering under God's Torah is not hers alone. The nations, too, come under the same Torah. As Paul proclaims, the sword of God is impartial (Romans 2:11; Galatians 2:6; Ephesians 6:9; Colossians 3:25) it bends Israel and the nations alike beneath the weight of his justice.

What the world calls justice is, in truth, unforgiveness. What God calls justice is mercy for the poor. In the Roman world, debt was treated as both a legal and moral obligation, with default viewed as moral failure and enslavement often the consequence. Wealthy elites presented this unforgiving system as righteousness. Paul's terminology of debt and slavery directly undermines this moralistic framework. He insists that the only true debt is to God, who paradoxically cancels debt through Christ (Colossians 2:14), and that true slavery is bondage to sin, while slavery to Christ is freedom (Romans 6). Unlike the Roman elite, Paul, following the Old Testament system of sabbatical and jubilee release (Deuteronomy 15; Leviticus 25), did not moralize about usury but instead exposed and undermined the smug self-righteousness of elites who justified themselves through debt enforcement. By redefining debt and slavery in divine rather than civic terms, Paul dismantled the Roman notion that repayment equaled justice and proclaimed God's justice as mercy for the poor.

Luke 8:39 - The Commission to Contested Territory

The Convergence of Three Itineraries

In Luke 8, when these arcs converge, the text itself sharpens like the blade of Ṣalāḥ ad-Dīn, keen, unyielding, and consecrated to divine justice:

- **מ־צ־א** (***mem-ṣade-aleph***), the man has been "found" by Jesus, restored to right mind and true allegiance.
- **ח־נ־ן** (***ḥet-nun-nun***), pleading to human powers is supplanted by faithful witness to God's mercy.
- **שׁ־ו־ב** (***šin-waw-bet***), he is sent back, not for reconciliation with the townspeople on their terms, but for confrontation on God's terms.

The Military Commission

> *ὑποστρεφε εἰς τὸν οἶκόν σου, καὶ διηγοῦ ὅσα σοι ἐποίησεν ὁ θεός.*
>
> *"Return to your house and describe what great things God has done for you." (Luke 8:39)*

When Jesus commands the formerly demon-possessed man to return ὑποστρέφω (*hypostrepho*) to his house, he follows the established pattern of prophetic commissioning. The command is explicitly military in character: Abrahamic in trust, Mosaic in intercession, Gideonic in courage, and Samsonite in confrontation.

The man's return is not prodigal but prophetic. He does not go back as one seeking reconciliation on the town's terms, but as a Pauline witness deployed into hostile territory on God's terms. His presence in the city becomes a standing rebuke to their cowardice, a living testimony of mercy refused, and judgment invited. In him, מ־צ־א (*mem-ṣade-aleph*), ח־נ־ן (*ḥet-nun-nun*), and שׁ־ו־ב (*šin-waw-bet*) converge as one commission: found, pleading rightly, and returned for confrontation.

The Geography of Confrontation

This hearing is reinforced by the geographical setting. The Decapolis—literally "ten cities"—functions as a visible marker of Greco-Roman imperial organization imposed upon Syro-Arabian nomadic lands. Within this context, Jesus' intervention destabilizes the symbolic architecture of empire: the name Legion evokes a Roman military unit; the destruction of the swine represents the loss of imperial property; and the fear of the population underscores their preference for imperial order over divine disorder and liberation. The episode thus dramatizes the tension between two competing allegiances: fidelity to Caesar and fidelity to God.

The fate of the swine is particularly significant. Their destruction signals condemnation of the people's alignment with imperial power. Both Legion and the swine embody allegiance to Caesar and Pharaoh. Both are manifestations of state authority and idolatrous domination. The crowd, in their collective rejection of Jesus and Moses, reveal their complicity in this order. Their insistence upon the stability of imperial slavery reflects a refusal to embrace the risk inherent in submission to God's word, a submission that, as the biblical wilderness tradition insists, often entails profound insecurity.

This is expressed rhetorically through the blasphemous language of the communal, tribal, institutional and familial "we." In human discourse, "we" masks an assertion of power under the guise of consensus or fellowship. When confronted with prophetic utterence, communities respond by appealing to collective identity: "We do not act in that way; we believe this; we have always practiced that." In this way, the communal "we" becomes a mechanism of resistance against the solitary divine call. It transforms rebellion into righteousness by granting disobedience the appearance of legitimacy through communal affirmation.

By contrast, in the Abrahamic tradition, there is only one true we: the voice of the Most High God. The human "we" is revealed as a presumptuous usurpation of divine prerogative, a communal voice that substitutes Caesar for Christ, community consensus for divine command, and group security for the radical solitude of standing naked before God.

The Qur'an makes this point with particular rhetorical force. The divine voice often speaks in the plural إِنَّا (*ʾinnā*, "Indeed, we"), or نحن (*naḥnu*, "we"), a usage known in Islamic tradition as the royal plural (نون العظمة, *nūn al-ʿaẓama*). Far from implying multiplicity in God, the plural underscores majesty and total sovereignty: God alone commands, God alone creates, God alone returns all things to himself. When the Qur'an declares, "Indeed, we sent down the reminder" (Qur'an, Sūrat al-Ḥijr سورة الحجر "The Rocky Tract" 15:9), or "We created man from a drop of mingled fluid" (Qur'an, Sūrat al-Insān سورة الإنسان "Man" 76:2), the plural serves as an intensifier, amplifying divine authority, in opposition to the human being, weaving the crimson thread sewn by the Torah and woven through the New Testament: man is not the reference!

This rhetorical strategy sets the divine "we" in stark contrast to the human tribal and communal "we." Whereas human assemblies invoke "we" to manufacture legitimacy—"we believe, we practice, we have always done"—the Qur'an insists that only God's "we" carries true authority. The human "we" is therefore a blasphemous echo, an idolatrous mimicry of divine majesty, masking disobedience as reference.

Seen from this perspective, the Lukan narrative is unmasked in the same light. The Gerasene crowd asserts its communal will in rejecting Jesus, but their "we" is exposed as false assembly, a swarm cicling death. Against them stands the solitary man, healed and commissioned, whose very presence testifies that the only true "we" belongs to God. His witness rebukes the false consensus of the city and embodies the obedience that the crowd has rejected.

The Absence That Exposes

In Luke's mashal, the return is marked by absence. The swine are gone. The crowd has dispersed. The man's former companions erased. He stands alone, found, and exposed with no community left to shield him, no filth left to conceal him, no power left to reference but the one who sent him.

This scene anticipates the final reckoning: the day when the disbeliever is given back his own deed, when tribe and city and oath dissolve into dust, and a man stands naked before the one who clothes him. This is the day that the Lord has made. To return is to step into that barrenness now, ahead of the Hour, with nothing in one's grasp but obedience.

Toward a Detheological Methodology

It is high time to disavow the Western psychological reduction of Scripture. The text is not about private piety, nor about cultivating interior states of repentance. It is about exposure: being cornered by what you are, found wandering in darkness with no means of self-rescue. Even the correct prayer is worthless if the one who utters it is corrupt.

In Luke, the healed man offers no temple implements, no sacrifices, no rites when Jesus finds him. Following the prophetic itinerary, the point is not human initiative; not searching, not pleading, not finding. There is no agency in securing mercy. The logic is inverted: you do not seek or supplicate; you are found. Mercy is granted when one submits, not when one acts.

Jesus sends the healed man back (ὑποστρέφω / שׁוּב / ث-و-ب) into the very city that had just rejected him. His commission is not dispersal but reinsertion into contested ground. It is Abrahamic in trust, Mosaic in obedience, Gideonic in courage, Samsonite in confrontation, Pauline in trajectory.

Across Torah, Gospel, and Qur'an, the prophetic return is one motion, seamless across traditions: to be found by God is to be sent by God, until the Day of the Lord, when the Lord's work find its own completion without human mediation.

Word From a Mother

"When the siege happened, it wasn't just a siege on the church itself. What they claimed was that there were some fighters that were in the church—which actually that's a Christian tradition, you know, for people to take refuge in a church. But the Israelis used that as a way to...well, they besieged the church. And the whole town was under siege, not just the church. So that meant that the teachers who lived in the Bethlehem area couldn't get out of Bethlehem to come over to Bethany. People couldn't get food and medicines. After a while, it became...I would get calls and saying, you know, my neighbor has epilepsy and we cannot get a new medication for her. Can you find a way to get something in, through a care organization, into us? And finally, when the siege ended—during that time, I remember a doctor telling me how someone had been shot in his house and he was bleeding to death. And he was calling the doctor, you know, what do I do? What can I do? And the doctor literally heard him just bleed to death during that, because no ambulance, nothing was allowed. And after the 40 days, roughly 40 days, which is ironic, I went in there and I met up with some of the people. Everything was strewn with garbage all over the streets, the bullet holes. You know, what Israel likes to do is destroy. Not only do they control the place, but they almost take glee. And we're not talking about Hamas time. We're not talking about, you know, 2023. We're talking about 2002. They would go through the town of Bethlehem and purposely, with their tanks—the smaller ones—knock over the light poles or the things that are garnished with Christmas tree decorations, and knock them over in the middle of town, or pull their bulldozer and smash a car. But again, that same resiliency of the Palestinians, the **ṣumūd.** *I have a photograph—he's actually the father of one of the priests now in Bethlehem—and he's sitting on his car that had been smashed by the Israelis, just with a smile, kind of like,* ***'You're not going to stop us. We're going to carry on. You did this***

to me, but I'm going to carry on.' *There were people shot inside the church. The bell ringer there was shot dead…and also a young 16-year-old boy who was an altar boy of the church…they were just kicking a soccer ball. He was shot dead by a sniper, 16-year-old Johnny Thaljieh. And also there was another—Christine Saadeh. Her father was the principal of the Orthodox school in Beit Sahour, Shepherd's Field. They were driving and the Israeli soldiers…mistakenly thought that was a car of some militant. So, they shot up the car. His wife was injured, he was injured as well, and his 12-year-old daughter Christine was killed. Why? What did they do wrong? They thought the Israelis thought that was somebody that was going to do something bad. Was anyone ever punished for it?"*[58]

[58] Mother Agapia Stephanopoulos. *"Here's What It's Really Like to Live as a Christian in the Holy Land."* Interview by Tucker Carlson, YouTube, uploaded by Tucker Carlson Network, August 15, 2025, www. youtube. com/ watch?v= y79CfG2R_3g.

"The lead guy, the guy in charge of the contract for UGS, Johnny Molford, is the Florida chapter president and national ambassador for the ***Infidels*** *Motorcycle Club. On his chest he's got a 1095 tattoo, which is the date of the first crusades, and their logo is a shield with a crusade cross on it.* ***Their emblem is the Crusader.****"*[59]

"I do not call this my story. I call this the story of the oppressed, the story of the Palestinians in Gaza who are dying at the hands of starvation and violence.

What I witnessed in Gaza, I can only describe as a dystopian post-apocalyptic wasteland. We, 'we', the United States, are complicit. 'We' are involved hand-in-hand in the atrocities and the genocide that is currently undergoing in Gaza. For anyone who says that there is no starvation or mass hunger… shame on you. ***Shame on you.****"*[60]

– Anthony Aguilar, Retired U.S. Army Special Forces Officer (Green Beret) and former contract security operator for UG Solutions at the Gaza Humanitarian Foundation distribution sites.

---

59 Anthony Aguilar, interview by Briahna Joy Gray, *Bad Faith Podcast*, episode 78, YouTube, 16 Aug. 2025, https://www. youtube. com/watch?v=-80CY_sceNE.

60 Anthony Aguilar, interview by Amy Goodman, *Democracy Now!*, "Fmr. Green Beret Who Worked at Gaza Food Sites Reveals Rampant War Crimes," YouTube, 15 Aug. 2025, https:// www. youtube.com/watch?v=57htMYk4UqM.

The Borderless Table

> *"They've all grown up together, the Christians and the Muslims. And there's a certain amount of commonality and respect. They can have their differences but overall the Palestinian culture is infused with both."*
>
> – *Mother Agapia Stephanopoulos*

The entry of Ṣalāḥ ad-Dīn into Jerusalem on October 2, 1187, scarcely twelve days after the siege began, was no accident of fortune. The city had been lost already on the summer slopes of Ḥaṭṭīn, where the Crusader host was shattered beyond repair. With the army gone, Balian of Ibelin abandoned the fiction of victory and sought terms. In 1099, the Crusaders had baptized the city in blood; in 1187, Ṣalāḥ ad-Dīn bathed it in Pauline mercy. Those who could pay were ransomed and released; those who could not were often freed under the standard of grace. *Eastern* (روم, *rūm*)[61]

[61] Romanides, John S. *Franks, Romans, Feudalism, and Doctrine.* Brookline, MA: Holy Cross Orthodox Press, 1982. Romanides argues that the Romans of the East were wrongly named "Greeks" or "Byzantines" by Western historians, erasing their identity as Romans (Ῥωμαῖοι / Rum): "The Franks reserved these names [Romania and *respublica*] exclusively for the Papal States and literally condemned the Eastern part of the Empire to be Graecia." In the East, however, Arab and Turkish peoples preserved the designation Rum, and Orthodox Christians were considered Romans. This supports the historical force of the title "Eastern Orthodox" (روم أرثوذكس / *rūm arthudhuks*), literally "Roman Orthodox," with *rūm* directly recalling the Eastern Roman legacy.

Orthodox Christians—whose long history in the Levant and enduring ties with the Muslim world he honored—were shown particular grace. That it occurred on 27 Rajab, the night of the Prophet's ascent (الإسراء والمعراج, *al-Isrā' wa-al-Mi'rāj*), gave the moment a sacred timbre beyond the reach of military victory.

> *Permeated even with Palestinian Muslim culture is the sense that Christians lived here and they recognize Jesus as a prophet. So, they respect him."*
>
> *– Mother Agapia Stephanopoulos*

This was not indulgence. Mercy was scriptural and Abrahamic strategy. Informed by his own early missteps in Egypt and shaped by the anti-Crusader intertextual currents of al-Andalus, [62] Ṣalāḥ ad-Dīn acted in

---

In the American context, however, Orthodoxy has been domesticated through Orientalist frameworks and consumer culture, producing what Mother Agapia has identified as an ambivalence toward Gaza. Such ambivalence is rooted in **internalized racism**, in which the children of Rum's and their converts' self-identity becomes entangled with a Crusader alignment for social and economic gain, ironically echoing the very patterns of power and self-interest critiqued by Paul in 1 Corinthians.

[62] Ṣalāḥ ad-Dīn's celebrated clemency was nurtured not only by Qur'anic and juristic imperatives of mercy but also by the wider interfaith intellectual climate of the Mediterranean. In al-Andalus, Jewish philologists such as Jonah Ibn Janāḥ developed a comparative Semitic philology in Judeo-Arabic that drew heavily on Arabic grammar while systematizing Hebrew (*Kitāb al-Tanqīḥ*).

continuity with a Levantine pattern—fragile but persistent—in which Jews, Christians, and Muslims shared streets, markets, languages, and Scripture. His restraint reaffirmed this deeper fabric, cutting off the root of vengeance before it could take hold.

ʿAyn taḥt ʿayn, "eye for an eye."

In this, Crusaders and Greco-Romans hear "justice"; but the desert hears mercy. Not vengeance, not philosophy, but restraint. A ceiling, not a license. A wound answered, then closed. Nothing more. This is not justice carved in the marble courts of palaces. It is Bedouin survival. If you do not stop the cycle, the feud devours the camp. So, you make a deal. You settle quickly. You move on. This is the scope of biblical mercy: not moral, not personal, not psychological or spiritual, but practical.

Jesus' point was precisely this: "You have heard it said, 'an eye for an eye...'" He was not overturning Torah. He was explaining it. Stop pretending justice belongs to you. There is no justice. Only God is Judge. You, men of dust, cut short your quarrels before they multiply. Do not strike again. Do not rehearse your grievance. *khalāṣ!*

This approach, carried forward by his successors and transmitted eastward through figures like Maimonides (1138-1204), fostered a culture of intertextual study and Abrahamic interconnectedness. These Andalusi traditions, absorbed into the Ayyubid domains by way of Jewish émigrés and their works, helped shape an ethos in which Ṣalāḥ ad-Dīn's policy of mercy toward Jews and Christians after the fall of Jerusalem can be understood. See Phillips, Jonathan. *The Life and Legend of the Sultan Saladin* (London: Bodley Head, 2019); Sáenz-Badillos, Ángel. *Comparative Semitic Philology in the Middle Ages* (Leiden: Brill, 2004); Stroumsa, Sarah. *Maimonides in His World: Portrait of a Mediterranean Thinker* (Princeton: Princeton University Press, 2009).

("enough", "cut it off")![63] Mercy in Scripture is not softness. It is discipline. It spares the camp. It spares the land. It spares you from yourselves. Ṣalāḥ ad-Dīn understood this and acted accordingly.

For the Muslim world, the recapture became an emblem of unity; for the Latin West, a shock that triggered the Third Crusade.

> *"In our school, we had icons which are part of the Orthodox tradition, pictures of saints and crosses in every classroom. No problem with that...the Muslim students and families embraced the nuns and the Christian teachers."*
>
> *– Mother Agapia Stephanopoulos*

---

[63] The expression خَلَاص (*khalāṣ*), from the root خ-ل-ص (*kha-lam-ṣad*) "to be pure, free, or released," carries a wide semantic range. In colloquial usage, it carries the function "enough," "stop," or "that's it," signaling completion or closure. It can also be directive ("cut it off") or ("finished/done"). In supplicatory contexts, it conveys "deliverance" or "save us," reflecting the sense of being freed. Cognates include *ikhlāṣ* (sincerity, purity of intention) and *takhalluṣ* (getting rid of something), all drawing on the same root notion of release and purity. The term is also used liturgically in the Rūm Orthodox tradition, as in the petition خَلِّصنا يا ابن الله (*khalliṣnā yā ibn Allāh*), "Save us, O Son of God." Here, salvation/victory is expressed not merely as rescue but as a decisive act of severance (for example, C.S. Lewis's *The Great Divorce*) to save us by cutting us off from that which enslaves or destroys. This usage resonates with Sūrat al-Ikhlāṣ (112), where the same root conveys uncompromising singularity and purity of God, a stance that implies *ṣumūd:* steadfast resistance through separation from idolatry and false attachments.

Equally practical, the scattering of Jews and Muslims after the fall of al-Andalus, too often told as exile and loss, is better understood through the biblical principle of divinely ordained scattering: a nomadic pastoralism that spreads the seed of instruction carried as the salt of Torah upon the earth.

> *"The land shall not be sold permanently, for the land is mine; for you are strangers and sojourners with me" (Leviticus 25:23).*

The Qur'an echoes this in the words:

> *"To God belongs the dominion of the heavens and the earth and whatever is between them" (Qur'an 5:120, Sūrat al-Mā'idah,* سورة المائدة, *"The Table Spread").*

This proprietorship of God admits no nationalism, for

> *"Indeed, the earth belongs to God; He causes to inherit it whom he wills of his slaves" (Qur'an 7:128, Sūrat al-A'rāf,* سورة الأعراف, *"The Heights").*

The intellectual and spiritual legacy of al-Andalus—Qur'an beside Bible, submission before Scripture, the Pauline discipline of table fellowship—did not die in Iberia. It was carried into the Ottoman lands, where it found stewardship. There, religious communities were not sequestered behind the rhetoric of "tolerance" but woven into a shared fabric of obligation and difference. This coexistence was not nationalist, but borderless, in keeping with God's claim of proprietorship over the earth (Psalm 24:1; Qur'an 2:284, Sūrat al-Baqarah,

سورة البقرة, "The Cow"). From Sarajevo[64] to Baghdad, Salonika to Jerusalem, neighbors traded in the same

---

[64] Even the Slavic provinces of the Ottoman lands preserve late echoes of the Levantine and al-Andalus tradition of coexistence and textual interchange. After the 1492 genocide in Spain, many Sephardic Jews fled to the Balkans, where Sarajevo in particular became a meeting ground for Muslims, Christians, and Jews under Ottoman administration (Cohen, Mark R. *Under Crescent and Cross: The Jews in the Middle Ages,* Princeton UP, 1994; Greble, Emily. *Sarajevo, 1941–1945: Muslims, Christians, and Jews in Hitler's Europe,* Cornell UP, 2011). In nineteenth-century Bosnia, the Franciscan friar Ivan Franjo Jukić (1818-1857) read the Qur'an in Ottoman Turkish and Arabic, sometimes with polemical intent but also with an ethnographic attentiveness to Muslim life, a gesture largely absent in the medieval Latin West, where Crusader polemic and anti-Semitism had foreclosed genuine interfaith study (Fine, John V. A. *When Ethnicity Did Not Matter in the Balkans,* U of Michigan P, 2006; Pinson, Mark. *The Muslims of Bosnia-Herzegovina: Their Historic Development from the Middle Ages to the Dissolution of Yugoslavia,* Harvard UP, 1996). By contrast, an Orthodox priest with nationalist aims, Mićo Ljubibratić (1839-1889), completed the first Serbian translation of the Qur'an, published posthumously in Belgrade in 1895 and based on French or Russian intermediaries (Kajkus, Hanifed. "Mihailo Mićo Ljubibratić: The Author of the First Serbian Translation of the Holy Qur'an," Rumeli İslam Araştırmaları Dergisi, 2021; "Qur'an Translation of the Week #89: The First Translation of the Qur'an in the Balkans," GloQur Project, 2022). His project was paradoxical: an attempt to render the Qur'an intelligible to Orthodox Serbs in the hope of uniting Bosnian Muslims and Christians under a Serbian national idea, a nationalist strategy set against the backdrop of the Ottoman Empire's own system of open but non-national coexistence. Likewise, in the early Yugoslav period, on the eve of nationalist and Zionist currents taking hold, the Bosnian Muslim orientalist Fehim Bajraktarević (1889-1970) undertook comparative study of biblical and Qur'anic texts, such as the story of Joseph/Yūsuf, within Sarajevo's interfaith intellectual circles (Filipović, Nedim. "Oriental

markets, broke bread across confessions, and studied their sacred texts not in isolation but in mutual recognition.

> *"St. Jerome translated the Bible in Bethlehem. His cells are under the Church of the Nativity. You know, the very roots of our Christian heritage are there—and we're letting it be destroyed."*
>
> – *Mother Agapia Stephanopoulos*

It was not the passage of time that dissolved this order, but Europe. The dismemberment of the Ottoman Empire after the First World War, the carving of mandates by Britain[65] and France, and the willing

Studies in Bosnia and Herzegovina," Prilozi za orijentalnu filologiju, vol. 1, 1950; Nathalie Clayer and Xavier Bougarel, Europe's Balkan Muslims: A New History, Oxford UP, 2017). That such encounters occurred at all, in a context marked both by the heavy hand of Orientalist categorization and the lingering shadow of Crusader polemic, underscores how the Levantine spirit of shared study, carried northward by Sephardic exiles from al-Andalus, continued to echo in Eastern Europe, even at the cultural edges of a continent otherwise defined by exclusion and rupture.

[65] McKernan, Luke. "'The Supreme Moment of the War': General Allenby's Entry into Jerusalem." *Historical Journal of Film, Radio and Television*, vol. 13, no. 2, 1993, pp. 169-180. McKernan's analysis of the official newsreel *General Allenby's Entry into Jerusalem* reveals that the "modest" entry on foot was a carefully staged performance, contrasting with Kaiser Wilhelm II's 1898 visit and intended to project moral authority. Multiple edited versions were distributed in early 1918, embedding Crusade iconography in visual propaganda. McKernan notes that while Allenby personally resisted being cast as a crusader, the event's cinematic framing,

complicity of Arab nationalists shattered the borderless way of life that had endured for centuries. Like their Western liberal counterparts, Arab nationalists were quick to invoke the record of Ottoman atrocities. From Sharif Hussein and his sons to the Arab, Turkish, and Greek nationalists of today, each, by exalting tribe and nation above borderless coexistence, became in effect the proto-Zionists (and now, crypto-Zionists) of the Levant: convenient instruments of the settled elites of the West, betraying the ummah for consumerism and false security, and in so doing, betraying God and his people:

> *"The Muslim world has been tested with the weakest, most corrupt, and most hypocritical scholars and rulers, because as a community our priorities have long been in the wrong place. After being ravaged by colonialism, we no longer rallied behind the core characteristics of true leadership: prophetic knowledge, principle, and integrity. We no longer valued what is just and true. We chased after the fickle mirages of autocratic power, wealth, charisma, and status. This was our downfall. As a result, we today see tight-lipped, impotent Muslim rulers idly watch the river of blood as it flows from Gaza. We see compromised scholars betray the Qur'anic command for justice and bend their heads in humiliation and fear of worldly powers. Save for a few, most Muslim rulers and scholarly elites have chosen self-preservation and silence. The river of blood in Gaza is also a river of treachery and collusion. With leaders like these, it is no wonder the Muslim*

---

combined with government and press narratives, made clear that Britain was strategically repurposing Crusader imagery to portray the conquest as both the culmination of a historic struggle and a moral triumph.

world is in the sorry state that it is in today. Palestinians could see from the very beginning that there is nothing 'post' about the postcolonial world order. They have ever since got less and less of their rights, lands, and dignity with each passing day. In the same era, the opium of nationalism spread like wildfire as the Muslim world was carved into colonial-constructed nation-states. The rest of the Muslim world enjoyed its false sense of sovereignty and accepted its bridle, divorced from the lonesome plight of the Palestinian people, fooled into believing that the same system that gave birth to their sovereign states could guarantee their safety and protection."[66]

Yet the matter at hand concerned neither the Ottomans nor, before them, the Umayyads, but the enduring reality of shared life: the legacy of Pauline table fellowship, preserved through the scholarship of al-Andalus and the everyday practice under the Ottoman domains. This is hardly an endorsement of the Ottoman Empire—still less of the Sublime Porte or the human reforms of Abdul-Mecid—any more than the letters of St. Paul were an endorsement of the Caesars, a common and careless error of Western colonial, dare I say Crusader, scholarship.

This fragile model of subsitance living, extinguished by Europe beneath the weight of an imposed, idolatrous national Alexandrian monotheism—a melting pot recast as the singular, dominant expression of white

---

[66] El-Sharif, Farah. *Sermons at the Court on the Chris Hedges Report: On the Arab and Muslim Betrayal of Palestine, "Systemic Sin" and the Future of Islam in the World. Sermons at the Court,* Substack, February 6, 2025, sermonsatcourt.substack.com/p/sermons-at-the-court-on-the-chris.

consumer monoculture. From Richard the Lionheart to mandate Damascus, the arc of erasure held unbroken. Its new emissaries, European generals, heirs to the Crusaders,[67] standing over Ṣalāḥ ad-Dīn's tomb and declaring: *"Saladin, nous voilà."*[68] [69] Its most recent

---

[67] Bar-Yosef, Eitan. "The Last Crusade? British Propaganda and the Palestine Campaign, 1917-18." *Journal of Contemporary History*, vol. 36, no. 1, 2001, pp. 87-109. Bar-Yosef demonstrates that, regardless of Allenby's explicit instructions to avoid religious language, the British government and wartime media apparatus actively framed the Palestine campaign as the fulfilment of medieval Crusading aims. Official propaganda invoked Richard the Lionheart, circulated *Punch*'s "The Last Crusade" cartoon, and spawned a wave of publications—*Khaki Crusaders* (1919), *Temporary Crusaders* (1919), *The Modern Crusaders* (1920), *The Last Crusade* (1920), and *With Allenby's Crusaders* (1923)—cementing the perception that 1917 represented the symbolic completion of the Crusades. Bar-Yosef concludes that this coordinated imagery shows the state's deliberate strategy to mobilize medievalist sentiment for imperial legitimacy.

[68] In French, "nous voilà" is an idiomatic expression meaning "here we are" or "here we come," often with a sense of arrival or confrontation. In this context, it carries a deliberate tone of triumphal return.

[69] Gabriel Puaux, Deux Années au Levant: Souvenirs de Syrie et du Liban (1939-1940) (Paris: Hachette, 1952), "Saladin, nous voilà"; as discussed by James Barr, "General Gouraud: 'Saladin, We're Back!' Did He Really Say It on Conquering Syria in 1920?," Syria Comment, May 27, 2016, https://joshualandis.com/blog/general-gouraud -saladin- back-really -say). Barr notes that Puaux's memoir is the earliest printed instance of the phrase—and likely reflects a later legend—and that if such a statement was ever made, it may more plausibly be attributed to General Mariano Goybet, who entered Damascus two weeks before Gouraud. For a contemporary eyewitness account, see Myriam Harry, "Le Général Gouraud à Damas," L'Illustration, no. 4045 (September 11, 1920);

enforcers in Gaza are American mercenaries, reminecent of the illiterate once drawn from Europe's peasant class, their bodies emblazoned with neo-pagan emblems of the Crusader armies.[70]

> "*Most of the population, most of the students are Muslims...the great danger is if the Christians continue to diminish, a key part of Palestinian society is lost. You go to Nazareth, you'll see many Catholic-run hospitals, schools—and so it's a fabric. It's a part of the whole character.*"
>
> – *Mother Agapia Stephanopoulos*

Where Scripture once governed the table (Acts 2:46; Galatians 2:12-14; Qur'an, Sūrat al-Māʾidah سورة المائدة "The Table Spread" 5:48), ideology enforced segregation; where the market once mingled the peoples (Nehemiah 13:16-22; Qur'an, Sūrat al-Ḥujurāt سورة الحجرات "The Chambers" 49:13), suspicion and checkpoints took root. The way of al-Andalus, scattered by God, preserved under Ottoman stewardship, was not extinguished by time, but by the deliberate will of Western powers. And yet, the record stands as testimony: another way was lived, in the shadow of

---

she reports that Gouraud did not enter the mausoleum, but sat outside under a lemon tree and made conciliatory remarks to local dignitaries.

[70] Anthony Aguilar, interview by Briahna Joy Gray, *Bad Faith Podcast*, episode 78, YouTube, August 16, 2025, https://www. youtube. com/watch?v=-80CY_sceNE.

Jerusalem's walls and in the breadth of the Ottoman domains. It can be lived again, for:

> *"To God belongs whatever is in the heavens and whatever is on the earth" (Qur'an, Sūrat al-Nisā'* سورة النساء *"The Women" 4:126)*

And:

> *"The earth is the Lord's, and all it contains" (Psalm 24:1).*

It can live. By his Command, what has been lost shall be found. What was buried shall be raised. What was forgotten shall be brought to light.[71]

---

[71] As Fr. Timothy Lowe has argued, the Greek imperative *Δεῦτε* (*Deute*, "come") in Matthew 4:19, corresponding to the Hebrew לֵךְ אַחֲרַי (*lek ʾaḥarai*, "go/follow after me"), should be understood not as an invitation but as a direct and uncompromising command. This usage echoes the divine injunction to Abram in Genesis 12:1, לֶךְ־לְךָ (*lek-leka*, "go forth"), both employing the qal imperative of הלך (*he-lamed-kaf*, "to go, walk"). Such imperatives highlight that discipleship, from its inception, is not a matter of voluntary association or religious sentimentality, but of radical obedience to a summons that leaves no room for hesitation. Lowe stresses that this command, when issued to Simon Peter, Andrew, James, and John, is universal in scope yet met with universally compromised hearers: Simon, "the stone," hears but fails to act; Andrew represents ὄχλος (*oxlos*), the generic "crowd" that in Matthew often embodies instability, susceptibility, and self-interest; James the supplanter embodies institutional ambition; and John alone signals hope in his name, "Yahweh is gracious." In this way, the Matthean command itself becomes the life-giving word: it dismantles human pretension, exposes fragility, and brings to light what was hidden, forgotten, or buried, affirming the absolute sovereignty of the divine summons.

As it is written:

> *"Whatever you have said in the dark will be heard in the light, and what you have whispered in the inner rooms will be proclaimed upon the housetops" (Luke 12:3).*

And again, the prophet said:

> *A voice said, "Cry!" And I said,*
>
> *"What shall I cry?*
>
> *All flesh is grass, and all its beauty is like the flower of the field. The grass withers, the flower fades, but*
>
> *The word of our God will stand forever."*
> *(Isaiah 40:6-8)*

صدق الله العظيم

God Almighty has spoken the truth.

Rise, Andalus.

RISE!

(Lowe, Timothy, *"An Examination of Discipleship in the Gospel of Matthew,"* 2025 OCABS Symposium, August 2, 2025, St Elizabeth Orthodox Church, St Paul, MN).

Word of the Three Scrolls

The word of the three scrolls is thus:
so long as the tent is widened,
it is not of the tribes;

So long as the word is held fast,
it is not of Alexandria;

Only then is there a chance—
when he utters his Name,
and you are no more.

Epilogue: Lift Up Your Gates

"The Prophet Abraham used to speak like this: 'O you wretched, insolent, conceited King, I did not send you to this world to collect worldly benefits. Rather, I sent you to respond to the supplication of the oppressed on my behalf.' And this is the exact opposite of what the Abraham Accords do: they strangulate the oppressed."

– Farah El-Sharif, Sermons at the Court

The Shepherd Returns

All of Scripture comes to this: hope and trust.
Not in the work of our hands, but in the righteousness of God.
He alone vindicates the poor; he alone tends the needy.
He is the Good Shepherd, the breath in the night,
the voice that calms the storm,
the hand that keeps the wolf at bay.

Will we close the gates?
Will we bind ourselves in chains?
Will we send him away?

To wait is to hope.
Yet waiting is also a test,
a scrutiny that ends in failure or in faith,
in ruin or in steadfastness.

Who can endure?
Who will remain when the King returns—

ignoring the mockery of nations,
turning only for his guidance,
submitting to his Command before the Hour,
trusting in the Day?

"Lift up your heads, you gates, and be lifted up you ancient doors, that the King of glory may come in. Who is the King of glory? The Lord strong and mighty, the Lord mighty in battle. Lift up your heads, you gates, and lift them up you ancient doors that the King of glory may come in. Who is the King of glory? The Lord of hosts. He is the King of glory." (Psalm 24:7-10)

Luke 8:40 - The Victor's Return

Καὶ ἐν τῷ ὑποστρέφειν τὸν Ἰησοῦν ἀπεδέξατο αὐτὸν ὁ ὄχλος· ἦσαν γὰρ πάντες προσδοκῶντες αὐτόν.

*"And as Jesus returned, the crowd welcomed [ἀπεδέξατο (*apedéxato*)] him, for they were all waiting [προσδοκῶντες (*prosdokontes*)] for him."*

Once again, these two terms—ἀπεδέξατο (*apedéxato*) and προσδοκῶντες (*prosdokontes*)—are not "meanings." They are functions. In Semitic lexicography, function always stands in opposition to meaning. Meaning belongs to narrative, and narrative is the machinery of propaganda, whether in antiquity or in the modern rhetoric of empire, from Greco-Roman polemic to the so-called "Abraham Accords."

Why call it propaganda? Because "meaning" is never an inherent quality of the word itself; it is always a projection of the interpreter's mind. Meaning is the phantom of temporality. The words of God, by contrast, are not subject to projection or temporality.

As Paul said:

> *"Now a mediator is not for one party only; whereas God is only one." (Galatians 3:20)*

And as the Qur'an repeats:

> *"Say: he is God, one." (Qur'ān, Sūrat al-Ikhlāṣ* سورة الإخلاص *"Sincerity" 112:1)*

God is one. He is permanent. Humanity, by contrast, is many and transient. This is why Paul's hymn in Philippians must be heard in functional, not metaphysical, terms:

> *"Who, although he existed [ὑπάρχων,* hyparchon*] in the form of God [μορφῇ θεοῦ,* morphe theou*], did not regard equality with God a thing to be grasped [ἁρπαγμός,* harpagmos*], but emptied himself, taking the form of a slave [μορφὴν δούλου,* morphen doulou*], and being born in the likeness of men." (Philippians 2:6-7)*

"Form of God" (μορφῇ θεοῦ, *morphe theou*) is not an ontological statement. It is a role, a functional designation. Christ bears this role as God's emissary, his proxy, just as Isaiah's Slave (עֶבֶד יְהוָה, *ʿebed Yahweh*) in 52-53 was despised, rejected, obedient unto death, and vindicated only after utter humiliation.

Paul does not speculate on what Christ "is." He testifies to what Christ did. Jesus did not grasp at power (ἁρπαγμός, *harpagmos*); he submitted. He obeyed. He became, in Isaiah's language, the מְשֻׁלָּם (*mešullam*), the one made whole through obedience, the one vindicated after surrender.

According to Paul, you might say: Jesus was the first-born of Gaza, the first-born of the the dead, the first to *submit.*

In any case, God's oneness—set over against human transience—exposes our impulse to do the opposite of Jesus: not to yield, not to submit, but to divide and then to conquer.

It is the same pattern repeated across the centuries. Since the seventh century, West Asia has suffered under this very impulse: fractured repeatedly at the hands of the Greco-Romans, and later, the Crusaders. Each imposed their divisions, their idols, their false unities, presenting multiplicity as though it were one: the so-called "melting pot," the imposed monoculture.

And the same violence persists today in the academy. Modern Western hermeneutics, clothed in the garments of scholarship, repeats the same Greco-Roman pattern. It fractures the text into competing "meanings," idolizes interpretation, and then enforces its divisions as though they were one: reception history, post-modernism, theological systems, ideological readings, etc., each another projection of the self.

Inevitably, this academic posture filters down into practice, shaping popular piety. Thus, we find movements preoccupied with "red heifers"[72] and other

[72] Evangelical Christian Zionists, beginning with Pentecostal preacher Clyde Lott in the late 1980s, have bred and exported red heifers to Israel in cooperation with the Temple Institute, believing their sacrifice, described in Numbers 19, will enable purification for the rebuilding of the Jewish Temple and hasten Christ's return.

spectacles, as though God's instruction were a ritual to be managed in service of empire, rather than the divine command to be obeyed.

Yet Scripture is clear: there is one God. And this God speaks with one voice, issuing one command. It is not yours. It does not emerge from you. It has been handed down to you in his words. The disciple, therefore, has only one task: to submit.

The Septuagint as Lexical Spine

Let me speak plainly, once and for all, about the Septuagint. For those who bow before identity and boast, "we have our book, and they have their book," hear the truth: the book does not belong to you. It belongs to him.

It is his scroll, rolled into three. The first was written in Hebrew, but even Hebrew was not born in isolation. It was created by the divine author out of the raw materials of the Semitic field, fashioned from the consonantal marrow of the Two Rivers region. From Akkadian to Aramaic, from Ugaritic to Phoenician, the triliteral system supplied the clay, but Hebrew was the vessel God himself fashioned from the grammar of his Command.

At the fountainhead of this functional grammar stands Ezekiel, who establishes the pattern of the scroll: "Son

---

This reflects the fusion of Western narrative theology/propaganda what Goodman refers to as "prophecy" and politics at the heart of Christian Zionism. See Goodman, Hirsh. "Forcing the End." The New Yorker, 20 July 1998; Spector, Stephen. Evangelicals and Israel: The Story of American Christian Zionism. Oxford UP, 2009; Sheizaf, Noam. "The Temple Mount Movement: Messianism and Politics in Jerusalem." +972 Magazine, 2013.

of man, eat this scroll…and speak" (Ezekiel 2-3). First קרא *(qārā', qof-reš-alef)*, "to call, proclaim, read aloud," then שמע *(shama', šin-mem-'ayin)*, "to hear, obey." The watchman's office (3:17), the temple measured (chs. 40-48), the bones made to hear the word and live (ch. 37)—Ezekiel codifies the lexical itinerary of Scripture: command spoken, command heard, command enacted. Ezekiel is "father" of Scripture not by metaphysical doctrine but by functional architecture.[73] His scroll is eaten, not analyzed; proclaimed, not theorized. That same architecture carries through the Septuagint's Greek and resounds again in the Arabic of recitation. Even the very name Qur'an (قُرْآن), from the root ق-ر-أ *(qāf-rā'-alif)*, mirrors the Hebrew ק-ר-א *(qof-reš-'alef)*, *qārā'*—"to call, proclaim, read aloud"—sealing the unity of the scrolls in the consonantal grammar of command.

This is why function, not meaning, governs Scripture. Meaning belongs to narrative; function belongs to command. As Tarazi never tires of saying, consonants and use—not metaphysical categories—carry the force

[73] Building on Tarazi's thesis, Nicolae Roddy identifies the Ezekiel school as a decisive force in shaping this scriptural trajectory, preserving and amplifying the prophetic message during the exile and its aftermath. Central to this process was the recognition that Israel's downfall did not result from the superior strength of its enemies but from its own misplaced trust in kings, armies, and fortifications—trust which the prophets consistently identified as idolatry. In its later stages, this same witness was sharpened by redactors operating within the Persian and Hellenistic milieu, who crafted the biblical canon as a polemical response to the political philosophy and theological pretensions of the Greek world. See: Roddy, Nicolae. *The Roots of Scripture: The Prophetically Influenced Priestly Critique of Human Institutions and Its Relevance for Today.* St. Paul, MN: OCABS Press, 2024.

of the text. Verbs like קרא *(qārā', qof-reš-alef)* and שמע *(shama', šin-mem-'ayin)* draw their weight from consonantal form and repeated deployment, not from later philosophical scaffolding. Likewise in Arabic, قرأ *(qara'a, qāf-rā'-alif)* and سمع *(sami'a, sīn-mīm-'ayn)* are not invitations to ontology; they are summonses to obedience. Scripture resists Greek speculation even when written in Greek; it presses language into the service of the Command.

Then it was rendered into Greek—not as a mere translation, but as the living, organic nerve center of Holy Scripture, the lexical spine through which the words of God interlock without us. Greek binds the Hebrew consonantal force into a shared lexicon, extending the Command across tongue and time. In *The Rise of Scripture* and *Decoding Genesis 1–11,* Tarazi underscores that Aramaic was the common spoken language in the Persian and Hellenistic periods when much of the biblical canon was finalized. This meant that scriptural diction had to resonate in a Semitic idiom even when rendered in Hebrew or Greek script. That is why canonical Hebrew and Greek texts sometimes reflect Aramaic structures or vocabulary. Even when Scripture was rendered into Greek—or, in the case of the New Testament, composed directly for Greek audiences—its canonical authority still derived from its Semitic diction and idiom, from Hebrew shaped in dialogue with the spoken Aramaic of the Levant. This linguistic soil ensured Scripture's unity, coherence, and resistance to Greek philosophical categories.

Alongside Hebrew and Greek, Arabic too takes its place in this divine economy. Together these tongues form the living matrix of God's instruction. The LXX was meant to be the gateway to the nations, a bridge to the anti-philosophical grammar of the Two Rivers region—hence the Greek New Testament. And in the same way, the Septuagint is also a lexical bridge forward, preparing the ground for the Noble Qur'an, which stands in continuity with this grammar as its third scroll, part of a unified Abrahamic system.

That is what the Septuagint is: a lexical key, an interface. To borrow the language of our age, the LXX is an API. Just as an API allows one system to connect with another, the Septuagint enables one scroll to be joined with another. It is the living bridge, the nerve center, through which the whole body of Abrahamic Scripture communicates.

And the fruit of this interconnectivity? Table fellowship—a fellowship not only of Moses and Jesus and Paul, but also of Muḥammad. This is the power of al-Andalus: not the monuments of Germanic, Umayyad, or Spanish civilization, but the table where the scrolls meet. A realization too often forgotten yet always awaiting remembrance. Forgotten by most, yes—but never by all.

And now is the decisive time, the critical hour, to recover our collective heritage: not as competing identities, not as tribes clutching at ownership, but as children of the Most High God.

So let us bow before him in the study of his words, in obedience to his Command, that we might sit together once more, under the palm tree, in fellowship, rooted in the same living nerve center of his three scrolls.

Dictionary Writing, Not Interpretation

In the case of ἀπεδέξατο (*apedexato*), we are dealing with a term whose itinerary lies strictly within the Greek text. Our task, therefore, is to trace that itinerary and assemble its usage. And remember, we are not interpreting. The study of God's instruction is lexicography: the defining of terms, not the speculating of philosophers. It is dictionary work, not the dabbling of the Socratic method.

The Abrahamic tradition is anti-Socratic. We are not gazing outward into the world, rummaging through "experience," trying to project meaning from the human being. **No.** We are submitting to what the text imposes upon us. We submit to the words of God precisely because they do not come from us. They are artifacts encountered upon us.

This is where Western hermeneutics goes astray. It begins with "meaning." And so, I repeat myself, because repetition is the path of the Abrahamic scrolls. I have said it before and I will say it again: not meaning, but function. Not meaning, but command. Not meaning, but submission. The Crusader presumes that human experience is the reference point, that truth is discovered through interpretation, through philosophy, through the speculative mind of man. That is the Socratic inheritance: question, interpret, synthesize, project. But Scripture tolerates none of this. Its words are not born of us; they confront us from without, pressing upon us realities we cannot invent or control.

Hear and understand: "human experience" as revelation is a fallacy. It is paganism dressed up as scholarship. It is idolatry under the guise of interpretation.

We labor not to trace how words are used in the chatter of men, not to chase how language shifts in culture, not to baptize the "evolution" of meaning in the name of scholarship. Language evolves? Who cares. We are not speaking of language. We are speaking of the words committed as they have been written in Scripture:

Words that belong to God.
Words that impose themselves upon us.
Words before which we bow down.

The scroll is eaten, not interpreted; spoken, not theorized. That same system binds Hebrew, Greek, and Arabic: Scripture resists philosophy and insists on obedience, pressing the disciple into the service of the Command.

ἀποδέχομαι (apodexomai) *- The Lexical Itinerary of Welcome*

ἀποδέχομαι *(apodexomai)*, is a compound. It is constructed from its usages in the text: at its base, to receive, to welcome, to extend hospitality. But the prefix ἀπό sharpens the deed. It does not merely mark reception; it intensifies it. It is decisive. It is acknowledgment that presses upon the ear: we are not talking about a social gathering or a dinner party.

Once again, we are talking about *submission*.

This kind of welcome is not casual recognition, not simple acknowledgment. It is an act of yielding. And that is how we must hear this term in Luke. Do not run to your dictionary. Follow the term's itinerary in the text itself. It begins with hospitality: Judith at the gates, the honor in Joppa, the joyful welcome of brothers in

Jerusalem, the acceptance of a report. The word's function then expands into acknowledgment and recognition: the acceptance of terms, the granting of petitions, the understanding of a matter, the admission of information.

It is a potent function that culminates in the acknowledgment of divine sovereignty.

So, what do we do with Luke 8:40? Will we trivialize it? Will we flatten it into, "they welcomed Jesus back"? What does that even mean? That nonsense comes from you. That is you giving an example about how everyone felt welcomed at your cousin's party. That is you turning Scripture into a lesson about "being nice."

But Luke is not talking about civility. He is talking about the **absence of you.**

The itinerary continues: cognitive recognition of reality on the ground, the lexicographical encounter with fact. Lexicography is the act of being overrun with reality, not fantasy. And yet, how swiftly it is diminished, reduced to a "Bible study" on "family values" and "hospitality," as though the text were written to reinforce our courtesies rather than to impose God's Command.

This term also carries the sense of formal acknowledgment, for example, public recognition offered in speech, proclaimed before all. In the New Testament, and especially in Luke, this word reaches its full significance once more in that most scandalous act, submission, this time, specifically to the divine words. In our day, we substitute softer expressions: "radical acceptance," "embracing reality," and the like. Call it what you will. But let us be clear: these are evasions. They are linguistic veils. You do not like the facts on the ground, so you dress them in gentler language to blunt their edge, to avoid the scandal of the command.

The text is unequivocal: bow down!

Words that expose the hypocrisy of civility.
Words that demand acknowledgment.
Words to which we must submit.

Against False Recognition

Those who receive the apostolic proclamation do not merely admit or recognize. Your recognition is not required. To interpret it this way is a mishearing of the word. On this point, so many stumble over the function of the term "amen."

Amen does not indicate, "I agree." Agreement, like recognition, is not required. The Most High God is not polling you for your opinion, your advice, or your vote. He is the Almighty God, the Terrible God, the Lord of Hosts, the King of Glory. He is not asking for your "amen" as recognition or assent.

Nor is he asking you to "catch up" with him, an impossibility. Still, you had better catch up before the Hour, before recognition of the Day, your deed in hand. That is precisely Paul's teaching: you are already caught in his net. Bad news for the French Existentialists, indeed. This is the scandal of grace. He has already claimed you.

The question is not whether you recognize it. The question is whether you accept it. Whether you submit to it. Because ultimately this function, this Greek term ἀποδέχομαι (*apodexomai*)—to welcome, to receive—is expressed in its fullest form as complete powerlessness before God. It is baptism: the yielding of the self to the one who has already claimed you.

The Itinerary Through Scripture

Take, for example, Judith 13:13: the function here is hospitality and reception:

> *"When they heard her voice, they hurried to the call of the elders of the city. They all ran together, both small and great, because it seemed unbelievable to them that she had returned, and they opened the gate and welcomed [ἀπεδέξαντο (*apedexanto*)] them."*

Here the function is associated with return, the act of receiving back into fellowship. Notice again how the word bends: return, repent. Everyone wants to play games with such terms. But this is not permissible. Theology is nothing more than the projection of the human mind, and there is no theology in Scripture. There is only function.

This is precisely what Jesus indicates in his teaching about the healed demoniac. Remove the demons, and there is hope. But introduce "theology," and you reconstruct worse demons still. You invite the demons back. You create false spirits, manufactured meanings, projections of the self, and the last state of that person is worse than the first (Matthew 12:43-45; Luke 11:24-26).

This is the trap of Western hermeneutics. You clear the house of one false hearing, and then you repopulate it with seven others: interpretive systems, theological constructs, ideological lenses. Each new meaning is just another demon, more dangerous than the last, because it arrives dressed in the garments of scholarship or religious ceremony. You call it interpretation, but it is possession.

The only hope is to remain under his control: under the control of God through his words, not yours. To stray from his words is to wander in the wasteland, without water, without shade. May I spend every breath as breath from the Shepherd:

Drinking the wind he gives,
Fed from the palm of his hand
By the pasture of his instruction.

To graze where he commands,
To drink where he opens the spring,
To rest where he plants his shade.

Consider 1 Maccabees 9:71, the acknowledgment of terms:

> *"Thus the sword ceased from Israel, and Jonathan lived at Michmash; and Jonathan began to judge the people, and he accepted [ἀπεδέξατο (*apedéxato*)] the situation at that time."*

Or 3 Maccabees 3:17, acknowledgment of petition:

> *"When the people heard this, they raised an outcry to heaven so that those nearby and those far away were astonished at the sound of their united cry. But the king, considering their unity, accepted [ἀπεδέξατο (*apedéxato*)] their plea."*

Or Tobit 7:16, acknowledgment of understanding:

"And Raguel called his wife Edna, and said to her, 'Sister, prepare the other room and bring her there.' She went and spread the bed with her for her, as he had said, and she brought her there, and she understood [ἀπεδέξατο (apedexato)*] the matter."*

Here the nuance shifts again: not just welcoming, but acknowledgment: terms, petitions, understanding.

Then 2 Maccabees 3:9, formal admission of information:

*"She told him about the great amount of money under the King's control, that Apollonius the governor had informed him; and Heliodorus went to the king and admitted [ἀπεδέξατο (*apedexato*)] what had been told."*

And 2 Maccabees 3:35, recognition of sovereignty:

*"And Heliodorus offered a sacrifice to the Lord and made very great vows to him who had granted him life, and he acknowledged [ἀπεδέξατο (*apedexato*)] the Lord of all."*

Here the progression sharpens: not merely human acknowledgment, but recognition of divine sovereignty.

Again, in 2 Maccabees 4:22, a collective welcome with honor:

*"And when he came into Joppa, he was welcomed [ἀπεδέχθη (*apedekthe*)] magnificently by the people."*

And in 3 Maccabees 5:27, the joyful acceptance of a report:

> *"But the Jews, as they heard this and perceived the invincible protection, praised the Lord who had so miraculously manifested himself, and they received [ἀπεδέξαντο* (apedexanto)*] the report with joy."*

Finally, in 4 Maccabees 3:20, the cognitive acknowledgment of reason:

> *"For since reason rules over the emotions, it is evident that the emotions are not destroyed; for if the emotions had been destroyed, it would not be possible for reason to recognize [ἀποδέχεσθαι* (apodechesthai)*] any of them."*

You hear how the itinerary unfolds: hospitality, acknowledgment of terms, petitions, understanding, admission of data, recognition of sovereignty, honor of the encampment, joyful acceptance, cognitive acknowledgment. Each stage defines the function and adds weight to the term.

And now hear Luke 8:40 in this light: Jesus returning to Galilee after sending his Father's instruction into the Decapolis, returning victorious from the mission. The crowd does not simply "welcome him back." They honor him. They acknowledge him. They submit to him. They receive him with the same gravity as those who recognize divine sovereignty, the same joy as those who perceive God's protection.

The itinerary outlined above puts "meat on the bones" of the function. The function becomes divine force. And the force points only to this: the return of the *locum tenens* of the King of the Heavens.

Words that open the gates.
Words that demand acknowledgment.

Words to which we must submit.

Acts and the New Testament Diptych

Now we come to Acts, which belongs to the New Testament within the Luke-Acts diptych. In Acts 2:41 the function is unmistakable: submission.

> *"So then those who had received [ἀποδεξάμενοι (*apodexamenoi*)] his word were baptized; and that day there were added about three thousand souls."*

Submission to the instruction in baptism. It is striking how, when one traces the itinerary of ἀποδέχομαι *(apodexamenoi)* across the canon, the trajectory itself makes the point: the term consistently intensifies from reception, to acknowledgment, to submission.

Then, in Acts 15:4: the honor of the encampment, the welcome at the tents. Here again, the function is acceptance, but not of the person, rather of the instruction. And here our modern world stumbles miserably. We want to sentimentalize the scene, to transform it into a lesson about "community" or "relationships." But no. This is not a kumbaya moment. It is not a gathering to pacify one another while the poor, Gaza, and all like them, remain unfed. To go about life speaking as though such things were not taking place—this is vileness beyond words. The words do not exist to name it.

> *"When they arrived in Jerusalem, they were welcomed [ἀπεδέχθησαν (*apedachthesan*)] by the church and the apostles and the elders, and they reported all that God had done with them."*

Lift Up Your Gates

Notice carefully: they did not gather to congratulate one another. They did not kumbaya. They did not form a parish council. They did not draft a five-year plan. They bore witness to what God had done. They reported his righteousness, not their own: those pointless, transient, polytheistic human deeds.

For his righteousness endures forever;
 their accomplishments fade as the grass of the field.
His word stands; their works wither.
His Command remains; their schemes collapse.

Record. Register what I am saying.

The Victor's Welcome

This is how one must hear: "And as Jesus returned, the crowd welcomed him." It is no polite reception. Jesus crossed the Rubicon. He commissioned the man, equipped him with the knowledge of his own deed, and sent him into the Decapolis, as I explained earlier. He turned his back on the swine and the unrighteous of Gerasa, and he returned victorious.

The gospel had been preached, and all the people bowed before him. When he returned, he received the honor of the encampment: the welcome at the tents. They submitted to the news, to the information, to the inescapability of the Command. They accepted. They acquiesced. And it carries a baptismal tone: the victory that comes not from them, but from God. It is his righteousness.

All of this lies in the itinerary of the term, which culminates in Acts, the second half of the Luke-Acts diptych.

It is all contained in the function of the word. And it is powerful.

The return is victory.
The return is conquest.
It is the conquering Jesus—
the Lord of hosts,
the Lord of Sabaoth,
the proxy of the Most High.

As the nations rejected God in his Son,
as the Greco-Romans turned away from his representative,
so this people bowed.
So this crowd accepted.
They opened the gate.
They welcomed him.
And in welcoming, they submitted.

προσδοκῶντες **(prosdokontes)*: The Test of Waiting***

"For they were all waiting for him."

Now, this second term is powerful. We must trace its Semitic itinerary: προσδοκάω *(prosdokao):* to expect, to look toward. This is the hope of Scripture. This is the test. To wait, but also to hope. To expect, to look forward. But remember: when you look, when you wait, you are being tested.

Everything in Scripture is double-edged, and the languages of the Semitic tradition preserve this tension. You cannot pin a term down and declare, "This is what it means." Not only because meaning is a projection of the human ego, but because in Semitic functionality—as in the proclamation of Pauline grace—the word itself is a sword of Damocles: always hanging, always cutting both ways.

The Noble Qur'an proclaims the same teaching: you are suspended, dangling from the very lips of God. You are caught. This is your Pauline fate: you are trapped, boxed in, without escape. You have nowhere to turn, save to submit to him.

The Divine Economy of Fate

You encounter him where you are found. Whatever your situation, whether with fortune or without, you are under God's judgment. You make do with what you have.

This is why people marvel at the ingenuity of the Gazans. They submit to him as they are found, and they endure. They make do, because they are held in the palm of God's hand.

You do not make excuses. Jerome, in his Latin rendering of the Psalter (*"ad excusandas excusationes in peccatis"*), warns against evil words, "to make excuses for excuses in sins." (Psalm 140:4; Vulgate) If you lack money and resources, you make do with the absence. If, by the will of God, you suddenly gain wealth, you do not sit back and relax. You work as hard as you did before, and harder still, "making the most of your time, because the days are evil." (Ephesians 5:16)

Which is why, in Semitic fate, Biblical and Qur'anic alike, it is dangerous to call wealth a "blessing." For to receive more is not permission to rest. It is a heavier yoke, a greater burden, more required of you:

> *"...but the one who did not know it, and committed deeds worthy of a flogging, will receive but few. From everyone who has been given much, much will be required; and to whom they entrusted much, of him they will ask all the more." (Luke 12:48)*

Indeed, the Hebrew root ק־ד־ר (*qof-dalet-reš*) gives us *qoder*, "darkness, gloom, heaviness", as in Job 6:16, where torrents "are turbid with ice, in which the snow hides itself," or in Psalm 42:10, where the psalmist laments, "Why must I walk in gloom [בְּקֹדֵר, *beqoder*] because of the oppression of the enemy?" Fate presses down like storm-clouds. To live under God's decree is to live beneath the weight of his judgment, where you, like Job, are found wandering in darkness.

The Greek term προσδοκᾶν (*prosdokan*), "to expect, to wait," carries the same burden. To wait in Scripture is never passive. It is to stand under trial. As its itinerary and usage demonstrates, to look forward is to be tested, to endure under scrutiny. Waiting in darkness is the biblical fate. Expectation is judgment. Hope itself is the Biblical heaviness of *qoder*, the Qur'anic decree of *qadar*.

Everybody dreams: "if I win the lottery, I can relax." This is Satanic fantasy. It is neither Scriptural nor Qur'anic:

> *"You fool, this night your soul is required of you" (Luke 12:20).*

To which the Qur'an adds:

> *"Then you will surely be asked that Day about pleasure." (Qur'an, Sūrat al-Takāthur* سورة التكاثر *"Rivalry in Worldly Increase" 102:8)*

What right have you to relax on the weekends as children go hungry? What right have you to call wealth "blessing"?

The prefix πρός (*pros*) heralds the warning:
you look ahead,
you lean into what is coming.
But what is coming?
Always in Scripture the answer is the same:
the Day of the Lord,
the Day of the Most High God.
And that Day is Judgment.

The day when tents collapse, when wealth is stripped away, when the desert yields nothing but the truth. The day when the herds scatter, when the encampments are overturned, when no banner of men remains standing. On that Day only his words endure, and before his decree, all must bow:

> *"Indeed, we sent the Qur'an down during the Night of Decree. And what can make you know what is the Night of Decree? The Night of Decree is better than a thousand months. The angels and the Spirit descend therein by permission of their Lord for every matter. Peace it is until the emergence of dawn." (Qur'an, Sūrat al-Qadr* سورة القدر *"The Night of Decree" 97:1-5)*

In the languages of God, the root ר־ג־ע (*reš-gimel-ʿayin*) speaks of his Command over time and turmoil.

As a verb, it names the One who רֹגַע (*rogaʿ*) the sea, stirring or stilling its waves (Isaiah 51:15; Jeremiah 31:35).

As a noun, it marks the fleeting instant, "For a רֶגַע (*regaʿ*) I abandoned you, but with great compassion I will gather you" (Isaiah 54:7; Psalm 30:6).

Regaʿ is pause, suspension, the brief moment in which God alone rules.

When the Scriptures were rendered as lexical spine into Greek, the sea's motion became ταράσσω (*tarássō*): to stir, to trouble.

And in Luke, the verb moves inward.

Mary hears the angel's word and διεταράχθη (*dietarachthe*) (Luke 1:29); she is "troubled," her heart agitated as the waters once stirred. Yet her functional *regaʿ* becomes the pause of obedience: the troubled instant turns into the womb of submission.

Zechariah, by contrast, is struck dumb "for a moment" (Luke 1:20), his voice suspended before the Hour, deed in hand until the appointed Day. His *regaʿ* is the silence that yields not to his own words, but to God's.

One stirred, the other stilled: together they embody the two poles of ר־ג־ע (*reš-gimel-ʿayin*): agitation and suspension, disturbance and pause. And this is the true *regaʿ*, the moment of divine sovereignty, the Night of Power!

But the Lukan counterfeit waits in Gerasa.

When the demons enter the swine, the herd "rushed headlong" (ὥρμησεν, *hormesen*) into the abyss (Luke 8:33). In a single instant, *regaʿ*, they are disturbed beyond recall, driven to ruin. Their plunge into the deep is an inverted baptism: not submission to him in death but collapse into the power of death under Caesar with Pharaoh; not cleansing, but contamination; not entrance into the flock but scattering into the abyss. Here the pause collapses—no Sabbath rest, no silenced suspension—only agitation without command, destruction without obedience. The swine are the distorted *regaʿ*, the instant of collapse.

In the Qur'an, the cognate ر-ج-أ (*rāʾ-jīm-hamzah*) takes the form إرجاء *(irjāʾ)*: deferral, postponement, respite.

Iblīs pleads:

> *"Grant me respite until the Day they are raised" (Qur'an, Sūrat al-Aʿrāf* سورة الأعراف *al-Aʿrāf "The Heights" 7:14–15).*

The unbelievers are warned:

> *"We grant them respite only that they may increase in sin" (Qur'an, Sūrat Āl ʿImrān* آل عمران *Āl ʿImrān "The Family of Imran" 3:178).*

Even the Prophet is told: "You may تُرْجِي (*turjī*) whom you will" (Qur'ān, Sūrat al-Aḥzāb سورة الأحزاب al-Aḥzāb "The Confederates" 33:51), you may defer, you may postpone.

Here the *regaʿ* is stretched, extended into history itself, yet always bounded by God's will.

Thus, the three scrolls converge on his lips:

- In Hebrew, רֶגַע (*regaʿ*) is a moment, and רֹגַע (*rogaʿ*) the stirring or stilling of the sea.
- In Greek, ταράσσω (*tarasso*) is the troubling of the heart before God's word, while ὥρμησεν (*hōrmēsen*) shows the corrupted instant of collapse, the inverted baptism.

- In Arabic, إرجاء (*irjāʾ*) is the deferral of judgment until the appointed day.[74]

All three preserve the same field: God's sovereignty over the instant.

He can shorten it to a breath,
stir it into unrest,
or stretch it into an age.

And when the pause is ended—
when Zechariah's mouth opens,
when the word to Mary's womb becomes flesh,
when the Spirit raises Jesus—
the silence and the stirring resolve into the Voice of the Shepherd,
calling his flock to hear.

---

[74] The doctrine of *irjāʾ* ("postponement") emerged in the late 7th and early 8th centuries during periods of political and theological conflict in early Islam. Its adherents, known as the Murji'ah, emphasized the deferral of judgment regarding a Muslim's faith or sins to God alone, especially in the wake of the divisive civil wars (*fitan*). For the Murji'ah, *īmān* (faith) resided primarily in belief, not in deeds, and questions of a believer's status, particularly whether grave sinners remained within the fold of Islam, should be postponed until the Day of Judgment. Their stance contrasted with the Khawārij, who declared grave sinners unbelievers, and with the emerging Sunni and Shiʿi orthodoxies, which integrated works more tightly into definitions of faith. See W. Montgomery Watt, The Formative Period of Islamic Thought (Edinburgh University Press, 1973), pp. 125-36; and Wilferd Madelung, The Succession to Muhammad (Cambridge University Press, 1997), pp. 27-30.

Our Semitic Roots

ע־ר־ף (ʿayin-reš-fe) / ع-ر-ف (ʿayn-rāʾ-fāʾ)

προσδοκάω (*prosdokao*) corresponds to ע-ר-ף (*ʿayin-reš-fe*), *yaʿarof*, "may it drip":

> *"May my teaching drip as the rain,*
> *My speech trickle as the dew,*
> *As droplets on the fresh grass,*
> *And as showers on the vegetation."*
> *(Deuteronomy 32:2)*

The same root, in Arabic ع-ر-ف (*ʿayn-rāʾfāʾ*) appears throughout the Qur'anic text in the sense of "to make known." In the purity of the Semitic languages, you cannot pin a function down: it resists reduction to a single "meaning."

In Arabic, ع-ر-ف (*ʿayn-rāʾ-fāʾ*) also carries the sense of "first rain," the gentle outpouring that breaks the drought, akin to the biblical image of the morning:

> *"He causes his rain to fall on the just and on the unjust" (Matthew 5:45).*

Rain and dew alike are signs of instruction and judgment, poured out without discrimination, given to all.

Thus, in the Qur'an, revelation is portrayed in precisely these terms:

> *"And he will admit them to Paradise, which he has made known [*عَرَّفَهَا, 'arrafahā*] to them." (Qur'an, Sūrat Muḥammad* سورة محمد *"Muḥammad" 47:6)*

Revelation is the gentle rain: it discloses, it makes known, and at the same time it grants entry into the Kingdom. And for whom? For those who are made righteous. How? Not by themselves, not by their own meanings, not by their own deeds, but by the instruction that comes from him.

ש־ב־ר (*šin-bet-reš*) / س-ب-ر (*sīn-bāʾ-rāʾ*)

The second Semitic function also correlates in Hebrew ש-ב-ר (*šin-bet-reš*), and in Arabic ص-ب-ر (*ṣād-bāʾ-rāʾ*):

> *"I hope [*שָׂבַרְתִּי, šabarti; šin-bet-reš*] for your victory* יְשׁוּעָה *(*yešuʿah*), O Lord, and I have done your commandments." (Psalm 119:166)*

This verse is often rendered, "I hope for your salvation." But that translation is misleading. יְשׁוּעָה (*yešuʿah*) is one of those Semitic terms that resists Hellenistic categories, whose functionality makes even the phrase "double-edged" insufficient.

When you hear salvation in English, you at once think of yourself. You imagine your holiness, your entry into Heaven, your personal "spiritual journey." Yet the text is not about you. It is neither post-modern, personal, nor received in history by your godless institutions. The key to hearing Scripture, always, is this: the absence of you. The Scriptural God is present in our absence, as The Poet wrote:

"I am not mine."[75]

Not just the absence of your tribe, your clan, your civilization, or your identity. **The absence of you**,[76] Ḥabibi.

All these things—tribe, clan, civilization, identity—are non-functional in Scripture. They are dust, passing shadows. Even prayer and praise are not captured in your tongues. Only in the languages of the text itself.

Even when you recite, "My mouth is filled with praise" (Psalm 71:8), you imagine that it is you who praise him. But Scripture allows no such conceit. You cannot praise him. If a word of praise is uttered, it is God who praises himself, until the end of the age.

Who gave you the utterance? Who placed the word in the Psalm and on your lips? Not you. Never you. It is written by him, for him, from him and through him.

And you still imagine it is yours?

You fool.

---

[75] Darwish, Mahmoud. *Mural* (1999, an excerpt). *Middle East Report,* no. 248 (Fall 2008), Middle East Research and Information Project (MERIP). Web.

[76] Darwish, Mahmoud. *In the Presence of Absence.* Translated by Sinan Antoon, Archipelago Books, 2011, p. 162: *"You and I are absent, you and I are present and absent. So, which of your Lord's favors do you two deny?"* In Sūrat al-Raḥmān (55), the repeated refrain functions as a *kairos*, a decisive moment, confronting humans and jinn with a choice. After enumerating God's blessings in creation—sustenance, beauty, and mercy—the surah compels the hearer to respond either with gratitude and submission or with denial and heedlessness. The relentless repetition underscores that every moment, and every sign within life itself, carries the double-edged Sword of the Spirit: submission or rebellion; mercy or wrath.

"And whatever good you have, it is from God." (Qur'an, Sūrat al-Naḥl سورة النحل *"The Bee" 16:53)*

"For from him and through him and to him are all things. To him be the glory forever. Amen." (Romans 11:36)

Which means that in Psalm 119 you are not hoping that God would hand you "salvation," as though it were yours to claim. That is the child's thought, the legacy of the Protestant Reformation. And yes—even if you are Catholic, even if you are Orthodox—if you live in the West, you are a child of that Reformation.

Everyone speaks about "their salvation" as though it belonged to them. A possession. A commodity. A product to be acquired on a Crusader's quest: wielded like plunder, carried like spoils, paraded beneath banners as though it were earned. You march as though into siege, storming Heaven as if it were a fortress to be taken by force and then display "salvation" like a trophy over the corpses of the poor.

But Scripture speaks otherwise. Salvation is not your conquest. It is not seized, bought, or won. It is his victory. His alone. It belongs to him for his honor, not to you for your boasting.

For he is אֵל קַנָּא (*'ēl qannā'*), "a jealous God." All worship, all honor, all glory belong to him. You cannot preserve his honor. You are dust, a failing breath, a passing shadow. You can only hope in him because everything rests on him:

He is the reference.
The circumference and the center.
The Alpha and the Omega.

Lift Up Your Gates

He alone bears the burden of his own Name.

So, you hope. "I hope." But do not confuse yourself with David. It is David who speaks in the Psalter. Not you, not me: David the King. And yet, even David is no king in Scripture. He is a shepherd. At best a prince, moving in riddles and dark sayings. But a king? No, not until he is rehabilitated eschatologically, in the Day of the Lord:

> *"I hope for your victory, O Lord, and I have done your commandments." (Psalm 119:166)*

The Etymology of Testing

The root ص-ب-ر (*ṣād-bāʾ-rāʾ*), in this sense of examining, of testing, is associated in the wider Semitic field, across the extant languages of biblical Hebrew, with the act of probing, even poking with a sword: testing, scrutinizing, sounding out.

Now, in this precise form, it does not occur in the Qurʾan. Yet within the Semitic tradition the semantic bridge is clear: probing and testing shade seamlessly into waiting and hoping. For to wait is itself the test. That is the "point." This is how the function of the root illuminates our hearing of the Hebrew text.

Both Hebrew and Arabic preserve this sense of probing or sounding out. Waiting is never passive. It is trial, endurance under pressure, scrutiny under fire. This is a critical emphasis in Scripture. Not only the Pauline ὑπομονή (*hypomone*), endurance, but the Semitic mechanism itself: the root, the function, the discipline of being tested by divine instruction. Paul emphasizes it everywhere because Scripture emphasizes it everywhere, and it breaks through in the Qur'an as صَبْر (*ṣabr*.) The same mechanism operating as the same grammatical function: ص-ب-ر (*ṣād-bāʾ-rāʾ*).

Lamentations spoke in the same cadence:

> *"The Lord is good to those who wait for him, to the soul who seeks him. It is good that one should wait quietly for the salvation of the Lord." (Lamentations 3:25-26)*

In spoken Arabic the root ص-ب-ر (*ṣād-bāʾ-rāʾ*) also pertains to the cactus, *ṣabr*, that thorny plant which bears fruit in the desert against all odds. The image is exact. Patience in Scripture is never passive resignation; as God himself prods, so too does the one who handles the thorny plant of instruction with their own hands, self-prodding, by God's own hand.

Like the cactus, the people of Gaza endure where no one expects life to endure. Yielding fruit in season and out of season, not according to their will, but according to his Command.

The force of this scriptural mechanism is that it mirrors life itself. Expectation exposes. To hope is to be sifted. Anticipation lays bare what lies beneath and what lies ahead. To wait is to stand fast under judgment. And this is why we live in the hope of the coming Kingdom, under the weight and pressure of the test. This is the marrow of true religion. Not the saccharine comforts packaged and sold in churches today, but the unvarnished artifact, the "brass tax".

And all of this comes to the fore in Luke's account of Gerasa. You wait upon Jesus as he returns from battle. This is the crucible of faith: the moment where anticipation itself becomes judgment. To wait is to be tested; to expect is to be exposed. This is what it means to be tried by the instruction: you endure until deliverance is revealed. In that endurance your hope is purified: not hope in yourself, not in your triumph, but in his victory.

Like the children of Gaza, you place all your hope not in princes,
not in chariots,
not in nations,
not in the powers of this world,
but in the victory of the Lord.

> *"Some boast in chariots and some in horses, but we will boast in the name of the Lord our God." (Psalm 20:7)*

> *"And victory is only from God, the Exalted in Might, the Wise." (Qur'an, Sūrat Āl 'Imrān* آل عمران *"The Family of Imran" 3:126)*

> *"Those to whom hypocrites said, 'Indeed, the people have gathered against you, so fear them.' But it [only] increased them in faith, and they said, 'God is sufficient for us, and he is the best disposer of affairs.'" (Qur'an, Sūrat Āl 'Imrān* آل عمران *"The Family of Imran" 3:173)*

It is the same vision that bursts forth at the end of the canon:

> *"And I saw heaven opened, and behold, a white horse, and he who sat on it is called Faithful and True, and in righteousness he judges and wages war." (Revelation 19:11).*

The returning Rider is the same Lord, the same Victor. His battle is his alone, his triumph his own. And your only part is to endure: to wait, to hope, to submit until his victory is revealed and Hind Rajab, and all those who have gone before her, are avenged.

This is salvation.
Not your possession.
Not your conquest.
But his Day.
The Day of the Lord.

The Nations' Twisted Waiting: Lamentations

There is another correspondence in Arabic, aligned to the Greek term προσδοκάω (*prosdokaō*), to wait, to expect:

- In Arabic: ق-و-ي (*qāf-wāw-yā'*)
- In Hebrew: ק-ו-ה (*qof-waw-he*)

> *"All your enemies have opened their mouths wide against you; They hiss and gnash their teeth. They say, 'We have swallowed her up! Surely this is the day for which we have waited; We have reached it; we have seen it.'" (Lamentations 2:16)*

Here in Lamentations, the nations gloat. They wait, but their waiting is twisted. ק-ו-ה (*qof-waw-he*) bends into schadenfreude. They delight in Zion's downfall: "Surely this is the day we waited for."

And yet the same Semitic root reappears in Luke's account of Gerasa, turned inside out. There, the nations drive Jesus away, gloating in his rejection. But the gospel calls for something else entirely. In the case of Jesus, to lift up the gates and welcome him as Lord, trusting him as Victor against impossible odds.

Lift Up Your Gates

This is the hope of Jerusalem: that in her lament, the Torah would be carried to Gerasa and all the nations.

This is the test of waiting, ק-ו-ה (*qof-waw-he*), does it bend toward destruction, or does it bend toward the Day of the Lord? Do you see the functionality? How it teeters, balanced precariously in the hand of the Shepherd? This is ק-ט-ה (*qof-waw-he*): you are suspended, caught between destruction and deliverance, between ruin and the vindication of the poor.

Now you tell me—
is there a difference?

Not in anticipation of others being crushed, O Pharaoh, but in hope for the vindication of the poor.

> *"Yet those who wait [*קוֹי, qowe*] for the Lord will gain new strength; They will mount up with wings like eagles, they will run and not get tired, they will walk and not become weary." (Isaiah 40:31)*

The Victory Welcome

Yes, they welcomed Jesus back as the Victor. For Jerusalem had been avenged in the hearing of the Torah against the wicked of Gerasa, the Greco-Roman tyrants. In Lamentations 2:16 the nations gloat over Zion's ruin. They open their mouths wide, hissing and gnashing their teeth. They boast and boast again: "Surely this is the day we were waiting for."

> *"And they planned, but God also planned; and God is the best of planners." (Qur'an, Sūrat Āl 'Imrān* آل عمران *"The Family of Imran" 3:54)*

Their waiting is a counterfeit, a twisted plot that delights in Jerusalem's ruin. Yet in the Qur'an the lesson of Lamentations is transposed and fulfilled. As it is written:

> *"If God did not drive back the aggressors [for all his people], the monasteries, churches, synagogues, and mosques in which the name of God is much remembered would surely have been destroyed. And God will surely support those who support him. Indeed, God is strong, [قَوِيّ* (qawiyy)*] exalted in might." (Qur'an, Sūrat al-Ḥajj* سورة الحج *"The Pilgrimage" 22:40)*

Here God, the master planner, does not gloat in Zion's fall. He drives back the aggressors for the sake of all his people—all of them.

Do you see it? Do you hear it? All who call upon his Name are gathered as one flock beneath the Shepherd. God himself preserves the monasteries, the churches, the synagogues, and the mosques where his Name is remembered. Where the enemies in Lamentations rejoiced at Zion's destruction, the Qur'an proclaims that God alone is strong to defend his worship and to protect the vulnerable. The Gospel of Luke resounds in the same cadence.

All of Scripture presses to this point: hope and trust. Not in the works of our hands, but in the righteousness of God.

He alone vindicates the poor;
he alone tends the needy.

Lift Up Your Gates

He is the Good Shepherd,
the breath in the night,
the voice that stills the storm,
the hand that keeps the wolf at bay.

So, I ask:

Will we close the gates?
Will we bind ourselves in chains?
Will we send him away?

To wait is to hope.
Yet waiting is never neutral.
It is a test, a scrutiny that ends in failure or in faith,
in ruin or in steadfastness.

Who can endure?
Who will remain when the King returns—
ignoring the mockery of nations,
heeding only his guidance,
submitting to his Command before the Hour,
deed in hand,
trusting in the Day?

The Church Will Not Abandon Her Children

جمعية القديس العظيم في الشهداء جاورجيوس

(jamʿīyat al-qiddīs al-ʿaẓīm fī al-shuhadāʾ jāwargiyūs)

Order of St. George[77] the Great Martyr
August 29, 2025

The following statement, dated August 29, 2025, commends the steadfastness of the Orthodox and Latin Patriarchates of Jerusalem for refusing to abandon God's people in the face of genocide, affirming that the Church remains steadfast in the hope of the Promise divinely inscribed: "God is not mocked" (Galatians 6:7). In the ancient churches and mosques of Palestine, displaced Gazans of all faiths, Muslims and Christians alike, seek and are offered refuge, as commanded.[78] *On this final point, it must be*

---

[77] In the Levant, al-Khidr, St. George, and Elijah are intertwined as later expressions of the ancient Baal figure, sharing dragon-slaying power, fertility symbolism, and overlapping sacred sites across Jewish, Christian, and Muslim traditions, with Elijah himself, as noted earlier, sustained by the *ʿarabim* (the nomadic people, the ravens, the Arabs). See Robert D. Miller II, *Baal, St. George, and Khidr: A Study of the Historical Geography of the Levant* (University Park: Eisenbrauns, 2019); and above, p. 160.

[78] "War Knows No Religion: Gaza's Oldest Church Shelters Muslims, Christians." *Al Jazeera,* October 16, 2023, www.aljazeera.com/ news/2023/10/16/war-knows-no-religion-gazas-oldest-church-shelters-muslims-christians. *Church of Saint Porphyrius.* Wikipedia, Wikimedia Foundation, last modified 2024, en.wikipedia.org/wiki/Church_of_Saint_Porphyrius. "Israeli Strike Hits Gaza Church, Killing 3 and Wounding Priest Who Was Close to Pope Francis." *AP News,* July 21, 2025, apnews. com/ article /3a53c 46a464 a7ef9d7 123bd ea6996d8a. "Gaza Church

affirmed with clarity: the credit rests not with the Christian patriarchies nor with their institutions, but with the Command itself. The land in which they dwell is not holy, nor are its shrines; it is, by all reckoning, occupied Palestine—under siege since the Crusades, yet, by the obedience of Ṣalāḥ ad-Dīn, a land for all faiths.

In the Name of the Father, and of the Son, and of the Holy Spirit. Amen.

The Holy Orthodox Order of Saint George the Great Martyr speaks with unyielding severity: Gaza has become a Golgotha of our age, and the blood of its innocents cries out to heaven while the rulers of this world drown it out with lies. We commend the Greek Orthodox Patriarchate and the Latin Patriarchate of Jerusalem, who in faithfulness to Christ have declared that they will not abandon their flock in Gaza City.

Within those sacred walls lie the starving, the elderly, the children, the disabled—the forgotten of this world. But they are not forgotten by us. They are not merely names on a list; they are our brothers and sisters, our friends and family, our flesh and blood. By refusing to flee, the Patriarchates have embraced the Cross, bearing witness to Christ Himself. Their courage condemns the cowardice of leaders who speak of order while

---

Opens Doors to Injured and Sick as Hospitals Fill." Reuters, 4 July 2024, www.reuters.com/world/middle-east/gaza-church-opens-doors-injured-sick-hospitals-fill-2024-07-04. "Gaza: Schools, Mosques, and Community Centers Used to House the Displaced." *Internal Displacement Monitoring Centre (IDMC)*, 2024, idmc.ajyal.ps/en/viewreport/oakaa-mrakz-ayoaaa-alnazhyn-fy-ktaaa-ghz-67e1da1f3e269. 2014 *Gaza War*. Wikipedia, Wikimedia Foundation, last modified 2025, en.wikipedia.org/wiki/2014_Gaza_War.

unleashing chaos, who praise human rights while crushing them beneath tanks.

Let it be said plainly: the announced plan to seize Gaza City and scatter its people is not war—it is eradication. It is not defense—it is desecration. It is not security—it is sin. To exile a people from their homeland is to spit in the face of the Creator. To bomb churches and starve children is to heap up curses upon your own heads. Those who design such evil, those who justify it, those who fund it—blood is upon your hands.

And we name the guilt: woe to the governments of the West, who arm this slaughter and then pretend clean hands. Woe to the leaders who send weapons and then issue hollow words of "concern." Woe to those who hide behind diplomacy while financing destruction. Woe to the powerful who place profit above mercy and alliances above justice. Your hypocrisy is as detestable as the cruelty it enables. You speak of international law while trampling it. You speak of peace while pouring oil upon the fire. You speak of morality while you barter away human lives.

The silence of your churches is no better. Those who fear to speak truth for fear of offense—your silence is betrayal. Every unspoken word condemns you.

Enough of the lies, the sieges, the massacres disguised as "operations," the starvation passed off as "strategy." The nations have chosen complicity; the leaders have chosen cowardice. The Order demands: stop this slaughter. Protect the sanctuaries of God. End the exile of Gaza's people. Free the captives. Feed the starving. Restore the dignity of every soul. Do not dare to speak of civilization while you permit barbarity. Do not dare invoke justice while you bankroll injustice.

Order of St. George

We declare before heaven and earth: the Lord of Hosts is not mocked. He who cast Pharaoh into the sea, who shattered Babylon, who struck Herod in his pride—He sees, He hears, and He will repay. Your thrones will fall, your power will rot, your nations will bear the shame of their complicity unless you repent. The blood of Gaza is upon you, and history will curse your names.

Saint George, who faced the dragon, did not compromise—he destroyed it. So too will the dragon of war, vengeance, and cruelty be cast down, not by the strength of armies but by the justice of Almighty God. Let all the world know: the Church will not abandon her children, Gaza will not be erased, the cries of the oppressed will not be silenced, and the God of Justice will have the final word.

The Order remains steadfast in its commitment to the community of Saint Porphyrios, to Archbishop Alexios of Tiberias, to the Greek Orthodox Patriarchate of Jerusalem, and to all Christians who live and breathe across Gaza, the Holy Land, Lebanon, Syria, Egypt, and the wider Middle East.[79]

---

[79] Office of Public Relations, *Order of Saint George*. "The Church Will Not Abandon Her Children." *Order of Saint George*, August 29, 2025.

From al-Andalus to Gaza: Scripture Against Empire

RISE, ANDALUS: THE FALL OF IMPERIAL HARLOTRY argues that the destruction of the shared Semitic intellectual tradition—rooted in triliteral grammar, comparative philology, and cooperative scriptural study—was the direct consequence of European imperial ascendancy after 1492. Through close linguistic analysis of Hebrew, Arabic, and Greek roots across the Bible and Qur'an, Marc Philip Boulos contends that the three Abrahamic scrolls function as a unified act of resistance against empire. The texts confront imperial systems not through philosophical abstraction, theology, or moral law but by exposing their hollowness and recalling humanity to a scriptural grammar of submission, difference, and encounter.

The book situates this argument within a historical arc stretching from the massacres at Acre and the Third Crusade, through the fall of Granada and the Alhambra Decree, to the Gaza Genocide of 2025. In each case, imperial violence is directed not only against peoples but against Scripture itself: an attempt to erase the Semitic memory embedded in consonantal language, prophetic confrontation, and the wilderness tradition.

Yet, the scattering of al-Andalus had a positive impact: its legacy of shared Semitic scholarship, inter-religious coexistence, shared living, and borderless table fellowship was carried into the Ottoman lands. There, diverse communities continued to trade, study, and live together under God's proprietorship, demonstrating that another way of life—Pauline Table Fellowship—was possible.

From al-Andalus to Gaza

Against this backdrop, Boulos emphasizes that true unity arises not from enforced sameness or ideological systems but from accepting divinely ordained difference and relinquishing self-reference. Drawing on the example of al-Andalus, where Jewish and Muslim scholars practiced cooperative philology, he highlights a model of textual interaction that resists domination while fostering shared submission to the Abrahamic word.

Ultimately, *Rise, Andalus* frames the Qur'an and the Bible as unified enduring witnesses against imperial domination and as pathways back to Jesus Christ through the shared Semitic roots of his Gospel. The book challenges Judeo-Christian imperial and pagan monoculture, while reclaiming the consonantal Judeo-Arabic grammar of Scripture as the living site of interfaith encounter, resistance, and hope.

About the Author

MARC PHILIP BOULOS is the author of *Torah to the Gentiles: St. Paul's Letter to the Galatians* and *Dark Sayings: Diary of an American Priest,* published through OCABS Press. He serves as pastor of St. Elizabeth Orthodox Church on St. Paul's West Side—the earth in which he was found and to which his voice returns. His writings and teachings unearth the roots of Scripture in Hebrew, Greek, and Arabic, tracing the Abrahamic roots of the Bible and the Qur'an. He hosts *The Bible as Literature Podcast* and edits the weekly Substack journal *The Voice of the Shepherd.*

Appendix: Hebrew Transliteration and the Palm Tree Initiative

The Consolation of Consonants

1. The Andalus Method

The transliteration of Hebrew follows a strict consonantal method, modeled on comparative Semitic philology and in continuity with the grammatical tradition of al-Andalus. The guiding principles are:

Consonants are primary; vowels are secondary. Vowels are written simply (a, e, i, o, u) without diacritical marks.

Bet (ב) = b, always b, never v.
Waw (ו) = w, never v.
Kaf (כ) = k, never kh.
Het (ח) = ḥ, never kh.
Ṣade (צ) = ṣ, never ts.
Fe (פ) = f, never p.
Shin (שׁ) = š.
Sin (שׂ) = s.
ʿAyin (ע) = ʿ. Always written.
Alef (א) = ʾ. Always written.
Qof (ק) = q. Never reduced to k.

For study, roots are always shown with dashes and spelled out by letter name:

מ־צ־א *(mem-ṣade-alef)*
ש־מ־ע *(šin-mem-ʿayin)*
ח־ר־ב *(ḥet-reš-bet)*

Words are transliterated plainly, with no intrusion of European orthography:

כָּתוּב *katub* not *katuv*
יִשְׂרָאֵל *yiśraʾel* not *yisrael*
דְּבָרִים *debarim* not *devarim*

This system eliminates the distortions of later Western or modern European conventions. There is no v, no kh, and no ts.

Arabic passages in this work are rendered in the standard academic transliteration system commonly used in Qur'anic studies and Middle Eastern scholarship (e.g., IJMES, Brill). This style employs macrons (ā, ī, ū) to mark long vowels, ʿ for the letter ʿAyin (ع), and ʾ for Hamza (ء).

Long Vowels (with macrons)

ā = long a (ـا, ا)
ī = long i (ي)
ū = long u (و)

Key Consonants (with parallels to Hebrew)

ʿ = ʿAyin (ع) parallels Hebrew ע (ʿayin)
ʾ = Hamza (ء) parallels Hebrew א (ʾalef)
ḥ = Ḥa (ح) parallels Hebrew ח (ḥet)
ṣ = Ṣad (ص) parallels Hebrew צ (ṣade)
ṭ = Ṭa (ط) parallels Hebrew ט (ṭet)

ḍ = Ḍad (ض) (no exact Hebrew parallel, emphatic d)
ẓ = Ẓa (ظ) (no exact Hebrew parallel, emphatic z)
th = Thā' (ث) parallels Hebrew ת (taw) in sound value
dh = Dhāl (ذ) parallels Hebrew ז (zayin) in sound value
kh = Khā' (خ) parallels Hebrew ח/כ in post-Biblical usage, where the Hebrew כ and ח often collapse into the same sound, rendered as kh. But in the Andalus system we resist this merger. Like "The Poet," we dwell in the palm of God's hand, exiled in the wilderness of Scripture, always absent in his presence. Thus, we keep the biblical distinction: כ = k, ח = ḥ.

As it is written:

يَا أَيُّهَا الَّذِينَ آمَنُوا كُونُوا أَنْصَارَ اللهِ كَمَا قَالَ عِيسَى ابْنُ
مَرْيَمَ لِلْحَوَارِيِّينَ مَنْ أَنْصَارِي إِلَى اللهِ ۖ قَالَ الْحَوَارِيُّونَ نَحْنُ
أَنْصَارُ اللهِ ۖ فَآمَنَتْ طَائِفَةٌ مِّن بَنِي إِسْرَائِيلَ وَكَفَرَتْ طَائِفَةٌ ۖ
فَأَيَّدْنَا الَّذِينَ آمَنُوا عَلَى عَدُوِّهِمْ فَأَصْبَحُوا ظَاهِرِينَ

yā ayyuhā alladhīna āmanū kūnū anṣāra llāh kamā qāla 'īsā ibnu maryama lil-ḥawāriyyīna man anṣārī ilā llāh qāla l-ḥawāriyyūna naḥnu anṣāru llāh fa-āmanat ṭā'ifatun min banī isrā'īl wa kafarat ṭā'ifa fa-ayyadnā alladhīna āmanū 'alā 'aduwwihim fa-aṣbaḥū ẓāhirīn

*O you who have trusted [of faith], be God's helpers (*anṣār allāh*), just as Jesus, the son of Mary, said to the disciples: 'Who are my helpers toward God?' (*man anṣārī ilā llāh*) The disciples said, 'We are God's helpers.' (*naḥnu anṣāru llāh*) Then a faction of the Children of Israel trusted, while a faction rejected. So, we reinforced those who trusted against their enemies, and they prevailed.*

(Qur'an, Sūrat al-Ṣaff سورة الصف *"The Ranks" 61:14)*[80]

REGARDING GREEK

For convenience and consistency, Greek vowels are plain. No macrons, no accents, no length markers, no diphthong diacritics.

α = a
ε = e, never ē.
ι = i
ο = o never ō.
υ = u (ου = u)
η = e (no long mark)
ω = o (no long mark)

Likewise:

χ = ch (never kh), φ = ph (never f), θ = th (never t), γ = g (always g, never gh or y), κ = k (always k, never c), ψ

---

[80] Personal conversation with Blaise Webster, March 20, 2025. Paul's use of συνεργός (*synergos*) in 1 Corinthians 3:9 is not a Greek philosophical coinage. In Diaspora Jewish texts such as Sirach and 3 Maccabees, συνεργός already functions in the sense of "ally in God's cause." Paul intensifies this usage, pressing the term into the anti-Hellenic soil of its Semitic background. When he declares θεοῦ γάρ ἐσμεν συνεργοί (*theou gar esmen synergoi*, "for we are God's co-workers"), the term resonates with the ع-ب-د/ ע־ב־ד (ʿ-b-d, "work, slave, worship") cognate branch, while the Qur'an's أنصار الله (anṣār Allāh, "helpers of God") aligns with the ع-ز-ر/ ע־ז־ר (ʿ-z-r, "help, support") network. Together with related Semitic roots that correspond via the LXX such as س-ع-د/ ס־ע־ד (s-ʿ-d, "support") and ح-ب-ر/ ח־ב־ר (ḥ-b-r, "companion, partner"), these terms form a broader Semitic constellation of "support, service, and partnership" oriented toward God's ultimate victory. Within this field, both Paul and the Qur'an depict humans as summoned to stand as God's allies, while God himself remains the true actor.

= ps, ξ = x, ζ = z, ρ = r (never rh), μ = m, ν = n, λ = l, τ = t, δ = d

2. The Comparative Frame

Hebrew transliteration is presented in dialogue with its Semitic siblings:

כָּתוּב (*katub*) parallels Arabic مكتوب (*maktub*).

מ־צ־א (*mem-ṣade-alef*) aligns with Arabic و-ج-د (*wāw-jīm-dāl*).

ש־מ־ע (*šin-mem-ʿayin*) resonates with Arabic س-م-ع (*sīn-mīm-ʿayn*).

ח־ר־ב (*ḥet-reš-bet*) corresponds to Arabic ح-ر-ب (*ḥāʾ-rāʾ-bāʾ*).

This comparative method situates Hebrew in its native linguistic ecology. It is not an isolated sacred tongue but part of a Semitic continuum.

3. Ibn Janāḥ and the Consolation of Consonants

The great grammarian of al-Andalus pioneered this consonantal method. In works such as the Kitāb al-Tanqīḥ ("Book of Exact Investigation"), he:

- Reduced Hebrew to its triliteral roots, mirroring Arabic philology.
- Used Arabic cognates to clarify obscure or rare Hebrew words.
- Demonstrated that the structure of Hebrew is revealed most clearly through comparative study.

Where Hebrew appeared ambiguous, Arabic provided consolation, illuminating the hidden consonantal grid and resolving uncertainty. This was the consolation of consonants: the comfort of clarity, order, and shared Semitic roots.

4. The Palm Tree Initiative

Our methodology follows the path of al-Andalus. By rendering Hebrew faithfully and placing it alongside Arabic and biblical Greek (the anti-philosophical Greek of Abraham), we:

- Preserve the consonantal backbone of the language.
- Resist modern distortions.
- Highlight the shared roots of the Three Scrolls.
- Continue the work of Ibn Janāḥ and the grammarians of al-Andalus, who understood that Hebrew is most alive when studied in its Semitic family.

This appendix serves both as a methodological guide and as a tribute to the Andalusian grammatical tradition, while offering a consolation to the present-day Levant in search of its roots.

By placing Hebrew, Greek, and Arabic side by side, this work seeks to extend that same consolation: to demonstrate that Abrahamic Scripture bears witness to a shared inheritance, a family of roots deeper than the divisions imposed by history, and to affirm a continuity across generations that resists forces of fragmentation and distortion, standing in opposition to the adversary.

www.ingramcontent.com/pod-product-compliance
Lightning Source LLC
Chambersburg PA
CBHW041538190426
43193CB00048B/2934
* 9 7 8 1 6 0 1 9 1 0 6 5 3 *